MW01252918

RISKS, IDENTITIES AND THE EVERYDAY

For Anna and Anne

Risk, Identities and the Everyday

16110

Edited by

JULIE SCOTT JONES
Manchester Metropolitan University, UK

JAYNE RAISBOROUGH
University of Brighton, UK

ASHGATE

Published by
Ashgate Publishing Limited
Gower House
Croft Road
Aldershot
Hampshire GU11 3HR
England

Ashgate Publishing Company
Suite 420
101 Cherry Street
Burlington, VT 05401-4405
USA

Ashgate website: http://www.ashgate.com

British Library Cataloguing in Publication Data
Risks, identities and the everyday
    1. Risk perception 2. Identity (Psychology)
    I. Raisborough, Jayne II. Jones, Julie Scott
    302.1'2

Library of Congress Cataloging-in-Publication Data
Risks, identities and the everyday / edited by Julie Scott Jones and Jayne Raisborough.
    p. cm.
    Includes bibliographical references and index.
    ISBN 978-0-7546-4861-1
  1. Risk taking (Psychology) 2. Accidents--Prevention. 3. Life skills.
    I. Jones, Julie Scott, 1969- II. Raisborough, Jayne, 1966-

    BF637.R57R575 2007
    155.9--dc21

2007031787

ISBN 978 0 7546 4861 1

Printed and bound in Great Britain by Antony Rowe Ltd, Chippenham, Wiltshire.

Contents

Notes on Contributors

Dawn S. Jones is a Senior Lecturer in Sociology at Liverpool Hope University. She has published in the areas of postmodernism; the tensions within Marxism and Feminism; and the relations between expert knowledge and risk perception. Her research interests revolve around the relationship between discourse, perception and reality. She is currently engaged in ethnographic fieldwork exploring women's perception of risk in pregnancy.

Lara Killick is a PhD student at Loughborough University, working under the supervision of Professor Joseph Maguire. Lara completed her undergraduate degree at Durham University, gaining first class honours, and then she spent a number of years living and working abroad. She returned to the UK in 2005 to complete her MA in Sociology of Sport at Leicester University. Lara's research interests are concerned with sport, health and risk; gender relations and the sociology of childhood.

Wendy Laverick is a Lecturer in Criminology in the Sociology Department at the Manchester Metropolitan University. Her current research interests are subsumed within the heading of transnational criminology as she extends her concern with violence and risk from an interpersonal to a global level.

Dave Merryweather is a Lecturer in Sociology and Identity Studies at Liverpool Hope University. His teaching and research interests are concerned with the experiences and perceptions of risk amongst young men and women in the course of their everyday lives. His most recent work focuses more specifically on young people's 'risk-talk' and how this contributes to the discursive construction, maintenance and problematisation of young people's gendered identities. He is currently undertaking a PhD with the Open University.

Jayne Raisborough is Senior Lecturer in the School of Applied Social Science at the University of Brighton. She has published in the areas of feminist theory, serious leisure and auto/biography as part of an overarching exploration of the contextual and emotional dynamics of identity and biography formation and risk. Her most recent work, with Matthew Adams, focuses upon the psychosocial relations of ethical consumption, 'taste' and class identity.

Julie Scott Jones is a Senior Lecturer in the Department of Sociology at Manchester Metropolitan University. She has published in the areas of American Christian fundamentalism and identity; secularisation theory; and social research methods. Her research interests focus on identity, worldview construction and meaning systems.

Sal Watt is a Lecturer in Psychology at Liverpool Hope University and Associate Lecturer with The Open University. Her doctoral research studied Civil Service 'culture' through the everyday experiences of civil servants, with specific attention to organisational 'risks' and Human Resource Management as a mechanism for change. Her wider research interests are drawn towards pedagogical debates and professional practice. Her most recent work focuses on the integration of study skills; action research and motivations for plagiarism.

Preface

This book has had a long and at times difficult gestation period. No fixed date can be given to its conception but its origins lie in long, in-depth and often heated discussions between colleagues in the department of Sociology at Liverpool Hope University. These discussions invariably took place during coffee breaks or in the less than salubrious settings of corridors. Such conversations were wide ranging but usually revolved around the same issues: identity, agency, risk, the self, and meaning. By the early summer of 2001 a group had come together, who decided to set down and explore some of these conversational themes in a formal sense. Many of the contributors of this book were part of this group, along with other colleagues from the Sociology department at Liverpool Hope University. Working papers were presented at a workshop series through the 2001–2002 academic year. The focus at that point was on the historical and theoretical: it was also overwhelmingly sociological in orientation.

In the 2002–2003 academic year, thanks to research funding from Liverpool Hope University, a formal Risk Research group was formed. This group's philosophy was to build on the field experience of most of its members, by focusing on applying risk theory to specific field settings and contexts. The group also wanted to explore micro risks within the everyday, and drew on a shared interest in Foucauldian analysis and Poststructuralism. From its inception the Risk Research group wanted to involve researchers beyond Liverpool Hope University and also from other academic disciplines. It succeeded: colleagues from Liverpool, Edge Hill, and Manchester Metropolitan Universities joined, drawing in people from Political Science, Social Policy and Criminology backgrounds. A seminar series was created, where formal, field research based papers were presented. The breadth of subject area; topicality; and the wealth of field data of the seminar series provoked the idea of this book and many of its chapters are based on papers initially presented at that time. The Risk Research Group's successful hosting of the BSA's Risk Study group annual conference, in 2005, allowed a forum for further critical comment on much of our work.

Some of the initial contributors have changed since the first book draft, but their input was invaluable. Similarly the inclusion of new contributors has added to the breadth and topicality of the book. This book is truly a product of collaborations over the past six years, both formal and informal. For this reason we would like to express our gratitude to the fortitude, energy, vision and at times sheer bloody-mindedness of everyone who has been involved in its creation.

Julie Scott Jones and Jayne Raisborough, 2007

Acknowledgements

Thanks are extended to the Department of Sociology at Manchester Metropolitan University and to the School of Applied Social Science at the University of Brighton for teaching relief and accommodation during the production of this text. We also gratefully acknowledge Liverpool Hope University who supported the founding of the Risk Research Group in 2002, and later hosted the British Sociological Association's Risk Research Group's Annual conference (2005) where many of these papers were first critically aired.

Chapter 1

Introduction: Situating Risk in the Everyday

Julie Scott Jones and Jayne Raisborough

The Everyday as Troubling and Troubled

The everyday has always been a focus of mainstream Sociology, particularly within the theoretical and methodological schools associated with phenomenology, symbolic interactionism, ethnomethodology, and ethnography (Berger 1967; Ritzer 1992; Denzin 1989; Layder 1994, 1997; Denzin and Lincoln 2000; Charon 2004; Cuff et al. 2006). What could be labelled a micro-sociological approach with its interest in the social actor, agency, meaning, and experience within the everyday has always been a strand of sociology, typically, contrasted with macro-Sociological approaches with their stress on structure (Berger 1967; Ritzer 1992; Layder 1994, 1997; Charon 2004; Cuff et al. 2006). These approaches sought to make the everyday 'exotic', 'contested' and not to be taken for granted (Berger 1967, 1991; Wright Mills, 1970). However, none of these approaches, typically, focused on exploring issues such as power that would fully problematise the everyday, although they did contribute by demonstrating how meaningful and relevant the everyday was and is for social analysis.

Feminist and poststructuralist sociological theories have made the everyday a far more problematic site than in the past (Evans 1992; Ritzer 1992; Ramazanoglu 1993; Layder 1994, 1997). By using the everyday, lived contexts of people's lives, the seemingly autonomous social actors of theorists like Goffman (1959) can be properly 'put in their place'. An example of this would be the Second Wave Feminist accounts that strove to name the once invisible yet materially sculpting forces of patriarchal power by critically charting the everyday worlds and lives of women (Friedan 1963; Rich 1979). It was in the mundane and commonplace that once secure sociological conceptualisations based on public/ private dichotomies were weakened. Liz Stanley (1988), speaking of the work/leisure dichotomy that served to underpin much leisure and work sociology, highlighted the political and conceptual importance of placing such terms in the *round* of women's lives, that is within the rhythms of women's socio-cultural realities of domestic and emotional labour that refused the 'neat' compartmentalisation of paid labour. The work/leisure dichotomy thus provided a wholly insufficient means through which to generate meaningful explanations for women's use, experiences and choices surrounding their leisure participation.

Poststructuralist analysis, which fed into and out of Second Wave Feminism, adds to potential analyses of the everyday, by introducing the concepts of reflexivity, subjectivity, discourse and resistance (Evans 1992; Ritzer 1992; Ramazanoglu 1993; Layder 1994, 1997). Drawing on the work of Foucault (1989, 1990, 1991, and 2003) in particular, the everyday is no longer 'just' the everyday world of the individual, but rather where identities, ideas of self, and discourses of power and control meet. One might argue that in the everyday, we see the real 'doing' of a society and thus by analysing the everyday we can explore key social issues. Gardiner (2000, 19) argues that there is, little 'that is natural or inevitable' about the everyday. Instead it is highly complex and processual; providing the temporal-spatial coordinates of our lived moments as they are shaped by daily negotiations and manipulations of contextual power relations. And it is this curious and shifting blend of the complex with the familiar that troubles the authority of theoretical assumptions (Foucault 1989, 1990, 1991, and 2003).

The construction of identity, specifically, can be explored via analysis of the everyday (Bennett and Watson 2002; Highmore 2002) and this is one aim of this book. In doing this we locate identities within the everyday world; a world that is late modern and dominated by risk. What we provide here is the location of risk in a range of everyday 'familiars' that are explored:

- *Familiar environments*: including, the school, the workplace, the antenatal clinic, the family, and the street.
- *Familiar preoccupations*: including, body image, career choice, 'hanging out' with friends, and playing sport.
- *Familiar social experiences*: including, becoming a parent, travelling, being religious, being a child, growing-up, and experiencing victimisation
- *Familiar social roles*: including, being a mum, being a child, being a student, being a young male, being a 'real' woman, and being a 'team player' at work.

If one wishes to explore identities as they are performed, constructed and defined in contemporary society, one must appreciate the conditions of late modernity and in doing so appreciate the role of risk discourses within it. It is here that this edited collection extends from the pioneering work of Deborah Lupton and John Tulloch (2001; 2002; 2003), who in response to the openings created by Beck's (1992) *Risk Society*, explored the meanings and perceptions people gave to risk as they recognised them in their own lives.

What emerged from their portfolio of work was that risks lay much closer to home that we had realised. Risks existed not just in macro systems of globalisation or world destruction to be avoided or reduced, but filtered down to frame key moments in the trajectories of people's everyday lives. Although risk cannot be isolated from notions of danger, hazard and threat in our cultural imaginary, similarly it could not be solely reduced to these; risks provided the opportunities, imaginaries and gateways for change and movement. It would be salient at this point to briefly review both Beck's (1992) and Tulloch and Lupton's (2003) model of risk, specifically as it relates to the individual and identity.

Late Modernity's Risky Problem

'Risk' has become a significant concept, and its incumbent theories, a crucial component of contemporary sociological analysis. Its centrality to much sociological theorising is illustrated by its presence in curricula and textbooks; a sure sign of a concept going 'mainstream'. Prior to Beck's (1992) *Risk Society*, an interest in and an analysis of risk was predominantly to be found in the domains of economics, finance, or in association with health and safety legislature. Although mention should be made to theorists, such as Douglas (1978; 1994), who in looking at ideas around illness, the body and purity boundaries, highlighted risk as an important consideration. That said, Beck's (1992) work represents the creation of distinct risk-theorising as a thing in itself within sociology.

Beck's (1992) work synthesised many related theoretical concerns that had been emerging within sociology in relation to late modernity. Late modernity represents a disjunction between the continuities and securities of modernity and the realities of the post-Second World War world (Giddens 1990). Modernity can be associated with rationality; fixed communal identities; grand claims to truth; Science dominated epistemologies; industrial-based Capitalism; the presumption of fixed and shared moral and cultural worldviews; and institutional solutions to society's ills (Beck 1992; Giddens 1990; Beck et al. 1994). However, beginning in the 1950s, and accelerating since the late 1970s, a number of emerging social, economic, technological, political, cultural and epistemological changes have emerged that have transformed society. These transformations have not only created what Beck calls the 'risk society', but have also precipitated a critique and challenge to modernity (Giddens 1990; Bauman 1992, 2001).

Late modernity is a period where 'meaning crisis' (Berger et al. 1974) is created through the critique of Grand Narratives (Lyotard 1984), such as Science, social institutions, institutionalised religion, and the idea of Society itself. This 'meaning crisis' exacerbates the individualism that was already an aspect of modernity, but goes further by unanchoring the individual from previously fixed communal or social-identities (class, nationality, gender, and so forth), which increasingly become contested within late modernity.

Economic trends that embrace neo-liberalist adherence to non-interventionist market policies and the move towards knowledge-based economic sectors, and away from manufacturing, make the world of world a more risky, competitive and isolating place for the individual (Beck 1992, Giddens 1991; Beck et al. 1994; Bauman 2001).

Politics is less interested in 'grand visions' for society, and more in surveillance and micro-management (Foucault 1991; Rose 1999; Bauman 2001). Technological advances mean that the mass media has become a key source of information about the world; this has been exacerbated by the decline in 'expert' knowledge caused by the critique of Grand Narratives previously mentioned. All these changes create a society with the heady cocktail of low levels of trust, high levels of insecurity, high levels of scientific and religious literacy and an almost omnipresent media: no wonder the individual in late modernity is susceptible to worrying about risk (Beck 1992; Beck et al. 1994). The late modern individual lacks the resources, solidarities and 'truths' that characterised that made the individual in modernity more secure and thus less prone to risk-anxiety. This is ironic given the fact that individuals living before the second half of the Twentieth century were much more prone to the everyday experience of disease, death and disaster. In other words risks have always been 'out there' in the form of famines, plagues, wars and so forth, but the late modern individual seems far more pre-occupied with them than past generations. For Beck (1992) and Giddens (1990) this shift has been caused by the decline in certainty or rather in what might be termed 'certainty-providers', such as Science, social institutions, or religion. But also, Beck (1992) asserts that the socio-economic and technological changes of Late Modernity create greater scope for risks, for example, environmental degradation, which are pernicious because of their global and universal impacts. For example, global warming affects everyone to some extent irrespective of class or status position.

Instead uncertainty dominates and when faced with perceived risks, such as environmental degradation or terrorism, the individual finds it harder to achieve ontological security (Giddens 1990, 1991; Bauman 2001). The media becomes a key conduit for risk-amplification, as individuals are overwhelmed by a constant stream of reportage, without the time or ability to 'think through' reported risks (Beck 1992).

For Beck et al. (1994:15), late modernity is a time he describes as 'reflexive modernisation', where individuals are left to construct their own identities or biographies. This occurs due to the creation of uncertainty within late modernity; individuals can no longer draw on established or traditional communal/social identities. Thus, individuals must fall back on to what they have left that is certain: themselves (Giddens 1991). Therefore late modernity becomes an era where the body and body commodification becomes extremely significant as a source for self-actualisation (Davies 1995; Du Gay et al. 2000; Pitts 2003; Jeffreys 2005), a theme that is explored by Raisborough in chapter two of this book. As individuals seek to construct their biographies, they rely on typically transient sources of identity, such as, self-help books, therapy, fashion, conspicuous consumption and dieting. The transience of such sources means that individuals never quite achieve full satisfaction with who they consider themselves to be, in other words the search for self-actualisation is ongoing and never-ending (Davies 1995; Du Gay et al. 2000; Pitts 2003; Jeffreys 2005).

Although Beck's (1992) analysis of late modernity is compelling, he is too focused on macro or structural level risks and this has been a key criticism of his work. He portrays the individual social actor as one who appears preoccupied by the next 'out there' risk, as defined by the media. But although such risks may have resonances with the individual to what extent might they be viewed in a fatalistic or even superficial manner? One can see this in the current debates concerning global warming: the risk is identified, it will affect everyone on the planet; and yet this has not led to widespread social movements or significant social action as Beck predicts (1992; 2002). Thus, there is then a suggestion that maybe macro risks are not the most significant in people's lives and certainly do not provide much impetus for identity construction. An additional criticism of Beck is his model of the rational social actor who is by nature risk-aversive (1992; Giddens 1991). This ignores the fact that for many individual the seeking out or embracing of risks may be a key source of identity construction (McNay 2000; Adams 2003; Brannen and Nilsen 2005) and that it may indeed be riskier not to embrace the risk in terms of group identities and statuses. In other words; socio-cultural contexts matter in relation to how risks are interpreted, and utilised by individuals. This is a theme that will be explored throughout this book, but especially in chapters two, four, five, six and eight.

Making Risk 'Real'

The work of Lupton and Tulloch (2001; 2002; 2003) represents the most significant attempt to tease out the complexities of the so-called 'risk society' that Beck (1992) neglects. Lupton and Tulloch (2001; 2002; 2003) incorporated three aspects to their work that pushes risk theory forward: they draw on empirical data, something Beck (1992) lacks; they focus on both the embracing and avoiding of risks; and finally they locate their analysis in the context of people's everyday lived experiences, what we might call the world of micro risks. Drawing on poststructuralist, in particular Foucauldian, analysis, Lupton and Tulloch (2002; 2003) focus on discourses of risk and relocate risk discourses back into an array of competing and inter-connecting social discourses. This approach involves viewing risks as discursive constructs that are heavily laden with values, meanings and cultural assumptions, regarding what is a risk and how one should act in relation to it (Tulloch and Lupton 2003). This discursive approach, following Foucault (1989), reconnects risk-discourses as one of a selection of competing discourses that involve and facilitate meaning, knowledge and control for the individual (Foucault 1989). Discourses establish social norms and realities, as well as subjectivities (Hall 1992; Foucault 1989). In focusing on participants' articulations of risk, Tulloch and Lupton (2002; 2003), present a more complex analysis of risk in relation to subjectivity.

At the heart of Lupton and Tulloch's (2002) analysis of everyday or micro risks is the 'voluntary risk-taker'. This is an individual who is 'reflexive' enough (a condition of late modernity identified by among others, Beck 1992; Giddens 1991; and Foucault 1989, 1990) to recognise risks but chooses to embrace the risk or, if you will, use it for the purpose of identity construction and self-development. Lupton and Tulloch (2002) found in their research that risk was pursued through a variety of means (including immigration, surfing, taking out a mortgage and riding rodeo), to seek excitement, self-improvement, achieve an 'authentic self', to take action and self-develop.

These 'voluntary risk takers' (Lupton and Tulloch 2002) draw on competing socio-cultural discourses and have to decide which ones 'work' for them in specific social contexts. Lupton and Tulloch (2002) also acknowledge that there are socio-cultural assumptions, for example gender, ethnicity and class, with respect to how individuals act in relation to risk in specific contexts. Drawing on the work of Foucault (1989, 1990, 1991), Lupton and Tulloch (2002) conclude that active, voluntary risk-taking functioned as 'practices of the self', affording self-actualisation, self-expression, and social progress. Lupton and Tulloch's (2002; 2003) approach to everyday risk is to be welcomed and this book certainly utilises their basic theoretical (poststructuralist, focus on the everyday, discursive analysis) and methodological (use of primary field data) approaches. However there are aspects of Lupton and Tulloch's (2002; 2003) work that remain under-theorised.

Firstly, although Lupton and Tulloch (2002) acknowledge that risk discourses emerge within specific socio-cultural contexts, locations and identities that work with or against other discourses, for example, gender and class, they fail to fully explore this issue. Risk, remains for them the key tool for exploration of the everyday. Risk does not operate as an external discourse, but as one embedded within the everyday; that operates both *by* and *through* other discourses. However, as all the chapters in this volume will demonstrate, risk can be a less important discourse in understanding individuals' actions, beliefs and behaviours. Age, class, gender, status, and family are all identified as central discourses that inform and mould individuals' identities and actions. One cannot understand the process of self-actualisation, merely by exploring risk as a lone discourse or behaviour. Risk is rarely the central discourse of self-identity, but rather a component or conduit of other more meaning-laden identities, for example, sexuality or class. For example, as Killick (chapter four) discusses in this volume, the discourse of the 'real' athlete means risking permanent injury, that may end a potential sporting career, rather than opting to 'sit it out' and wait for the injury to heal. 'Real' athletes do not 'sit it out'. Thus, in the context of the school environment where children are aspiring to the status of 'real' athlete, this risk taking behaviour is only made sense of in relation to the discourse of 'real' athlete. In other words the risk discourse does not operate alone, as a thing in itself, external to the context. Following Foucault (1989, 1990, 1991, and 2003), discourses work together and against each other, bound within specific contexts, to construct realities and subjectivities.

The second key aspect of Tulloch and Lupton's work (2002; 2003) that can be criticised and that this volume seeks to address is the issue of 'choice'. Lupton and Tulloch's (2002) 'voluntary risk taker' is one who actively chooses to seek out or pursue risks. But the notion of 'choice' is conceptually intertwined with neo-liberal ideas of independence and empowerment (Epstein and Steinberg 1998; Jeffreys 2005), that can lead to a lack of critical appreciation of the specific material and cultural conditions in which so-called 'choices' are offered and made (Brannen and Nilsen 2005). This model of the seemingly autonomous social actor ignores the fact that individuals are enmeshed within specific socio-cultural contexts (Foucault 1989, 1990), where normative codes of behaviour operate to reinforce specific hegemonies of power. In critically examining 'choice', this volume will explore how 'choice' becomes illusory in many risk discourses and that the social actor may indeed have no 'real' choice at all. For example in both Raisborough (chapter two) and Merryweather's (chapter five) respective chapters, gender emerges as a key discourse that in specific contexts restricts choice and enforces compliance through risk-taking behaviours, such as cosmetic surgery and the misuse of alcohol. When relocating such risk discourses and behaviours within specific gender orders and regimes, one realises that in the 'choice' between conformity to normative behaviour codes and assuming a 'deviant' identity, the loss in social terms would be too great to countenance anything but compliance.

In addition, moving away from a focus on 'choice' towards a more context-driven analysis, one may explore the morality of 'choices'; in other words 'choices' bring with them incumbent codes of right and wrong, duty, responsibility, respect and status. In looking at the moral aspects of 'choices' one can begin to appreciate the pressures asserted on individuals within specific communities or sub-cultures to participate in behaviour mainstream society may designate as 'risky', 'deviant' and possibly 'immoral'. This is especially demonstrated in Laverick's (chapter six) powerful chapter on violent offenders. Mainstream society may deem violence as 'immoral' and may see violent offenders as individuals who make a 'choice' to utilise violence; but by exploring family and community contexts alongside gender, class and race discourses a clearer picture emerges as to why some individuals and communities normalise violence. In such communities to take the morally 'right' path, as defined by the mainstream, would be to possibly lose personal status and also to make you vulnerable to victimisation.

Exploring the Everyday: Our Approach

Drawing on the work of Lupton and Tulloch (2002; 2003), this volume seeks to develop themes that they have left under-explored and unproblematised; including the criticisms discussed in the previous section. One of the strengths of their work has been the use of empirical field data, which has always been a central criticism of other risk theorists, such as Beck (1992). Theories can only be meaningful if applied or analysed in the light of empirical data and therefore all but one of the chapters in this volume draws on a range of field data, typically, qualitative. There has been no deliberate attempt to impose a specific method or methodology upon the contributors, but the use of participant observation, interviews and focus groups predominate. All the contributors work within the range of methodologies which could be labelled phenomenological, i.e. concerned with the lived experience, meaning construction and individual interpretation (Berger 1967; Ritzer 1992; Layder 1994, 1997; Charon 2004; Cuff et al. 2006). This would seem the most pertinent methodological approach when attempting to explore the 'everyday'. There was also a desire to explore a range of different social milieu and experiences, that offered an opportunity to investigate different social identities in different 'everydays'. In this volume childhood, adolescence and young adulthood are explored; the body emerges as a key source of identity and risk; gender and class are presented as still crucial markers of identity; and the workplace, the family, and the school sports field are all presented as contexts filled with risk choices.

Theoretically, all the contributors to this volume have theoretical leanings that can be broadly placed under the heading of Foucauldian influenced poststructuralism. Foucault contends that identity becomes fluid, always contested, possibly problematic and always context bound. Within that context discourses apply to identities and define them, problematise them and so forth. Individuals are active social actors, who use reflexivity as a tool to orient themselves around the discourses that circle them. Individuals cannot stand outside of these discourses but are bounded within discursively constructed contexts. Thus individuals construct subjectivities through the acceptance or resistance of discourses that seek to impose hegemonic order upon social worlds (1989, 1990, 1991, and 2003). For Foucault (1989, 1990) this sense of 'choice' is restricted through the operation of hegemonic codes of behaviour and discourses of surveillance and control; but the individual can become empowered through 'small' resistances. One good example of this is in relation to risk. In this volume Scott Jones (chapter eight) explores the use of long-term independent travel as a discourse for negotiating adult identity, which can offer temporary resistance to, while posing a critique of, consumer society. For the young adults featured in that chapter, the risks of 'losing out' on the career ladder, debt, or travel-related dangers, are a means to 'resist' discourses of consumerism, conformity and class, and thus offer a means for empowerment to individuals who feel disempowered by socio-economic realities. One of the criticisms (Hall 1992) of Foucault is that in his theory of discourse, power and subjectivity, the mechanisms by which subjects are constructed in and through discourse or how they are able to resist the imposition of discourses remains under-developed. So Foucault provides a useful analysis of how the individual negotiates various power/knowledge regimes but the issue of how and why individuals may invest in or reject such discourses remains unanswered. Lupton and Tulloch (2002) also fail to fully account as to why some individuals invest in certain discourses, while others are able to resist. In this volume the contributors attempt to explore this issue, through the locating of discourses of risk, identity and power; and in analysing the meanings participants' attribute to each. For example, in Jones's (chapter three) chapter some mothers-to-be elect to take genetic tests, while others reject them. In order to understand each woman's choice, attention needs to be placed within her own experiences, knowledges and wider socio-cultural contexts.

A Foucauldian influenced model of the self is the model central to this book. Beck's (1992) and Giddens' (1991) model of the social actor is of a rational social agent. Thus this model cannot accommodate social actors who may seem irrational by their pursuit of risks, which bring danger (but also potential pleasure and excitement), for example binge drinking, bungee jumping, or extreme sports. Lupton and Tulloch (2003) present a similarly rational model of the social actor, but one who is reflexive enough to rationalise what might be seen as irrational behaviour to others, through discourses of excitement, action, or self-development. We follow this approach, but further contest the very nature of what is rational. Poststructuralist analysis would suggest that 'rationality' is an extremely contested term, and needs to be socially and culturally contextualised, something Lupton and Tulloch (2002) do not do. In this volume, as with the issue of 'choice' discussed earlier; what is rational needs to be contextualised amidst competing socio-cultural discourses and specific group identities. To illustrate, in Laverick's (chapter six) chapter individuals choose to engage in violence, including murder, to prevent bullying and other forms of victimisation. Looking from outside the social context of these individuals' lives, it would seem irrational to commit violence as it brings with it moral condemnation and legal sanction. In addition, many outside this particular social milieu would see pre-emptive violence as morally wrong and something which could be 'fixed' with recourse to specific legal or social care agencies. However, Laverick contends that for those within this social milieu, violent pre-emption is the only rational choice if one wishes to avoid victimisation, maintain status and gain a sense of self-empowerment.

As well as a focus on the discursive construction of subjectivities and identities, Foucault (1989, 1990) also presents a framework for exploring the construction of reality, specifically of the everyday. By locating, competing discourses, normative codes of practice, and hegemonies, one can view meaning construction and interpretation, in action, for a given context. As with identity, Foucault (1990) suggests that meaning and the everyday are problematic and open to change and contestation. Poststructuralist frameworks necessarily harness both structural and cultural imperatives and our use here is to tease out discursive formations of risk, their reproduction, resistances and relations. However, a defamiliarising task is in operation as we each approach these normative processes that help constitute the familiar of the everyday and offer some explanation for why these take hold as they do. How meaning is constructed and reality interpreted is specifically explored in the chapters by Jones (chapter three) looking at antenatal genetic testing and the construction of a scientific 'reality'; Watt (chapter seven) looking at the interpretation of workplace 'behaviours'; and Scott Jones (chapter eight), which looks at young adults' attempts to construct a 'different' adulthood.

Risk, Identities and the Everyday: The Case Studies

The first case study presented in this book, in chapter two, stands out from the other case studies as it does not draw upon primary field research. Instead Jayne Raisborough effectively utilises popular cultural resources, such as advertising, television, and self-help books to explore the increasing normalisation of cosmetic surgery. Increasing attention has been given to the fact that cosmetic surgery, once the domain of fading movie stars and millionaire's wives, has gone 'mainstream'. As Nevin (2006) notes Britons last year spent over £600 million on cosmetic procedures. Recent populist surveys of young British women have shown that the majority would rather be thin than successful in their careers, and even more startling the majority of female graduates would prefer a breast enlargement to a first class honours degree! As Raisborough notes popular 'makeover' shows, such as *You Are What You Eat* and *Ten Years Younger* (both broadcast by Channel Four) reproduce a discourse that equates a 'better body' with a 'better life'. But as Raisborough highlights, most of the focus on cosmetic surgery has been on the 'risks' around having elective surgery. Raisborough's chapter focuses instead on the relationship between risk and discourses around the 'ideal' body and gender identity. Raisborough challenges Lupton and Tulloch's (2002) model of the 'voluntary risk taker' by exploring the way that discourses of the 'ideal' body relate to women's lived experiences and self-image. The risk to have cosmetic surgery is a lesser one than having an 'imperfect' body. Thus Raisborough explores what she calls the 'conditions of choosing' that women negotiate. In doing so, Raisborough also problematises Lupton and Tulloch's (2002; 2003) model of 'choice'; do women, particularly as they age and develop 'imperfect' (read old) bodies really have much of a choice to resist the ever more powerful discourses of consumerism, youth, femininity and the 'ideal' body that revolve around cosmetic surgery? Raisborough suggests that cosmetic surgery falls into a continuum of beauty driven bodily alterations, from waxing, corset wearing to foot binding that have always existed to make women conform to normalising discourses of femininity, desired sexuality and powerlessness. Raisborough sees an analysis of risk as a useful tool in exploring these issues.

The remaining chapters of this book draw on case studies based on primary field data. These chapters are presented in an order that takes the reader through the various transitions of the life course, from childhood to adulthood. In chapter three, Dawn Jones explores, through focus group research involving a group of mothers-to-be, the difficulty of being a mother-to-be in a world dominated by risk-assessment. The chapter specifically looks at antenatal genetic testing, an area of medicine that has grown in significance over the past twenty years. Motherhood itself has increasingly become identified as 'risky': as a possible career-wrecker or at least not compatible with a successful career; as a financial drain in this world of conspicuous consumption and consumer debt; or as a place of blame where all society's ills are posited, from childhood obesity to anti-social behaviour. Yet despite such 'risks'; motherhood and the mother-child bond is still culturally idealised, and mothers are still esteemed as protectors of their children; a protection that starts from conception. Mothers, who do not fulfil this protector role, for example by drinking during pregnancy, can expect to feel the full force of society's moral unease. With advances in our knowledge of antenatal care and the developing needs of the foetus, risk discourses continue to grow in relation to pregnancy and what women should or should not do with respect to diet, exercise and so forth. Jones acknowledges that despite the increasing distrust shown towards scientific discourses and knowledge in late modernity; in some realms of social life we still defer to Science as an objective 'truth'. Jones found that antenatal testing is one of those areas. The women in the study had to negotiate powerful moral discourses which focused on the need (economic, social and cultural) to have a 'perfect' baby. The medical discourses around the objectivity and accuracy of the antenatal tests fed into these moral discourses to assert pressure and anxiety on to the women. Ironically, as Jones notes, by agreeing to such tests, the women risked having their pregnancies labelled 'at risk' (of having an 'imperfect' baby), which in turn ruined the 'authenticity' of the experience for them. For the majority of the women 'facts' (i.e. the test results) were a better choice than 'fears', but in making that choice the experience of becoming a mother was ruined and impacted on their future roles as mothers. Many of the women decided that any subsequent pregnancies would go ahead without antenatal genetic screening so that the women could experience an authentic' (read here 'fear free') pregnancy. But as Jones notes, although the women sought information from non-medical sources (such as the Internet, friends, and magazines) to inform their choice of going ahead with testing, such sources were always seen as secondary to the privileged and institutionalised knowledges of medical 'experts'. Thus pregnancy remains a locus for divergent risk discourses that can only continue to develop as genetic testing becomes more sophisticated. Such discourses have important consequences for women and their experience of motherhood.

Green and Singleton (2006) argue that despite an informed concern with risk in the Social Sciences, there is still little empirical work that explores the voices and experiences of young people and the ways in which they manage and experience risk in the working of their everyday lives and spaces. Chapters four (by Lara Killick), five (Dave Merryweather) and six (by Wendy Laverick attend to this with different emphasis in this collection.

Children become the focus of chapter four, which draws on Lara Killick's fieldwork amongst child athletes. As Killick acknowledges, much has been written about sport and identity, but the focus has been predominantly on adult experiences.

Similarly, although risk discourses permeate throughout the world of sport, especially around injury assessment, again the focus has been on the world of adults. Taking risks and risking injury has always been part of the construction of 'real' sportsmen and women; a fundamental aspect of the sporting 'great', perhaps. But do aspiring child athletes see risk around injury in the same way? Childhood is increasingly defined and constructed around risk discourses, particularly risk-prevention. From diet, playground games, to school trips; children's lives are seen as potentially risky and thus must be protected and controlled (Palmer 2006). However this has led to a certain amount of over-proscription of children's lives and has launched the recent 'death of childhood' debate (See for example Palmer 2006). Ironically, Killick demonstrates that although life away from the sporting field might be controlled and highly risk-aversive, the opposite is true on it. The young athletes in this chapter demonstrate the same risk-embracing behaviours of their adult counter-parts: indeed to sit out a game due to injury is to 'risk' not being seen as a 'real' athlete. Instead the children would rather risk further physical damage to their bodies in order to validate an identity as a 'proper' athlete, who heroically plays through the pain. In contrast to Jones's (chapter two) where pregnant women deferred to medical 'expert' knowledge; the children in Killick's study deliberately ignore or challenge 'experts', such as doctors, coaches and parents who try to make the children 'rest' an injury. Killick concludes by noting that sport may be a useful forum for children to assert an identity and to seek personal empowerment. Such empowerment may be an increasingly useful tool for children in the ever more proscriptive world of childhood.

Dave Merryweather's chapter (chapter five) moves further along the life course to adolescence and specifically male adolescence among working class youths. Whereas Raisborough's chapter (chapter two) focused on discourses of gender and risk, Merryweather's chapter looks instead at masculinity, and it should also be noted he combines his gender analysis with one on class. Adolescence, like childhood, is increasingly associated with risk discourses; and male teenagers specifically are the focus of much 'concern' around anti-social behaviours, such as over-consumption of alcohol, drug misuse, and violence. Merryweather's focus group of male teenagers demonstrates that powerful discourses of masculinity, sexuality and class work to construct and control identities. As Merryweather notes a simple focus on the material practices of risk taking, such as, binge drinking, will not give a full account of why young males participate in such behaviours. Similarly, such behaviours may appear irrational to someone external to the group; but within the group they are fundamental components of being and belonging. To not participate in a fight would be an irrational choice as it would lead to masculinity being challenged and thus make group membership precarious. Again the issue of choice emerges: is there a real choice for such teenagers, in the face of family, communal and gender identities? Just as Killick's (chapter four) child athletes attempted to reject 'expert' advice, so too did Merryweather's teenage boys. They knew that teachers, doctors and so forth were 'right' to say do not drink, smoke, have casual sex, and so forth; but that the act of rejecting such knowledge and power discourses presented a source of empowerment and self-actualisation that helped to facilitate identity construction.

In chapter six, Wendy Laverick focuses on the centrality of context for understanding people's lived experiences of risk. Laverick draws on interviews conducted with violent offenders of both genders. Again gender and class prove to be significant discourses, as do ethnicity and family environment. Violent offending is condemned in mainstream moral and legal discourses. Yet, as Laverick highlights, many communities utilise violence as an everyday fact of life and tool for self-protection and self-empowerment. Just as Merryweather's (chapter five) teenagers could not be understood outside of their specific gender and class contexts, similarly, Laverick argues that violent offenders' lives need to be contextualised within specific socio-cultural milieus. Typically, risk management discourses within the criminological and legal domains focus on how to manage or design-out violence within specific communities. However, this is predicated on a rational, risk-aversive model that sees violence as something that is universally deemed to be morally 'bad' and the domain of 'last resort' behaviour. Laverick demonstrates that for some individuals, families and communities, violence is the only 'choice' and to not fight back might actually be seen as 'irrational' as it opens one up to potential victimisation. Additionally, the ability to fight may offer routes to self-actualisation and empowerment, especially for women. In this regard Laverick's chapter presents important new data regarding women and the use of violence, not as a 'last resort' but as an active, deliberate strategy for self-protection and empowerment. Laverick's chapter demonstrates how specific communities can normalise violence to such an extent that the individual who chooses not to fight back becomes a 'deviant' to be labelled and bullied. Thus, again the issue of 'choice' is problematised: does the violent offender really have a choice to not fight in a socio-cultural context where an ability to fight determines one's status and identity? It is only when removed from such contexts that Laverick's interviewees could reject the violent strategies of their earlier pre-incarceration lives; but all acknowledge that such violence was a fundamental survival strategy and source of status and identity within their families and/or communities.

Chapter seven reviews another arena that is filled with risk-management theories: the world of work and specifically human resource management. As Beck (2000) notes the world of work, within late modernity, becomes increasingly riven with insecurities, due to specific economic and technological changes. Such insecurities are spread throughout the economy, making the notion of a 'job for life' increasingly remote. Whereas in the past jobs in manufacturing were more prone to job insecurity; today even what were once perceived to be secure, middle class jobs are now seen as vulnerable to technological and economic trends. Yet as Sal Watt highlights, little research has been done into how workers, particularly white collar workers, deal with and respond to workplace uncertainty. The rise in workplace uncertainty has gone hand in hand with the growth of management strategies that seek to make workforces 'service-driven' and 'customer-focused'. Such strategies play on contemporary discourses of consumerism and individualism. These forms of personnel management often change with prevailing trends in human resource management theorising and can lead to staff having to deal with such regular changes to practice. Sal Watt draws on data collected from ethnographic field research in a Civil Service department. Little external research has been done on the experiences of civil servants and in this Sal Watt's work makes a valuable contribution. The Civil Service is a good case study to explore risk discourses and job insecurity as it has endured decades of 'modernising' initiatives, while simultaneously facing budget and staff cuts. The civil servant no longer has a taken for granted 'job for life'. Watt's demonstrates that the civil servants are forced to comply with the Human Resource Management (HRM) discourses that define and construct their work environment. Those that choose not to comply face several consequences including; risk rejection from the 'family-like' discourses of their work-teams; be seen as letting everyone down; or not being seen as committed enough. Again, the issue of 'choice' emerges and the civil servants must choose which risk is worse, for example to not work longer hours and risk being seen as not 'committed' within the institutional setting or to work longer hours and risk an impact on family life. Like Merryweather's teenagers in chapter five, group identities and memberships are constructed in resistance to authority based discourses of 'experts' or institutions. In other words, Watt's found that the civil servants in her study saw their existing team spirit and cohesion as 'authentic' and grounded in communal practice and Civil Service history. In contrast management imposed HRM discourses of 'family', 'team' and 'professionalism' were therefore doomed to fail as they were seen as external, imposed from above, not rooted in Civil Service 'culture' and therefore inauthentic. But as HRM becomes a vehicle for organisational change and adaptation in an increasingly uncertain work environment, Watt notes, that resisting HRM discourses and not embodying them into civil servant identity may result in increasing insecurity as the Civil Service is seen as unwilling to change. If Governments see the Civil Service as 'outdated' or resistant to change then further HRM initiatives will be launched and further rationalisation of the Civil Service will be initiated; creating even greater job insecurity and risk.

The final chapter, chapter eight, focuses on young adulthood and the perception that 'adult' is an increasingly contested and precarious identity. Scott Jones draws on focus groups that explored middle class university students' perceptions of 'growing up'; the meaning of adulthood; and the problems of making the transition into 'full' adulthood. Scott Jones identifies an emerging definition of adulthood that is marked by economic status and success, and that is increasingly devoid of the social statuses, roles and responsibilities that once were associated with adulthood. But this economic model makes adulthood a more problematic status for individuals to attain, dependent as it is on successful economic participation.

Adulthood has become an increasingly problematised identity and status, due to specific socio-economic trends and the emergence of a risk-preoccupied 'therapy culture' (Furedi 2004). Both serve to prolong the dependence young adults (those aged eighteen to thirty) have on families, other care-givers, and specific institutional settings. These young adults, like Jones's mothers-to-be in chapter three, Merryweather's teenagers in chapter five, and Watt's civil servants in chapter six, all face a transition in status that is vulnerable to risk discourses. Scott Jones highlights those current socio-economic trends, such as, high levels of personal debt, graduate unemployment and rising property prices that act to 'defer' adulthood for those who should be entering it on graduation. Thus, young middle class adults are faced with remaining in a 'deferred' state of transition, with its incumbent identity and status crisis, or a choice to 'opt out'. Media discourses played a key role in moulding the students' perceptions of 'deferred' adulthood as a risky enterprise, with little room for reassurance. The students regarded remaining in this state of 'becoming' as more risky than 'opting out'. Again we see the issue of rationality being context driven: it might appear irrational for a graduate to embark on a period of long-term, independent global travel rather than pursue a career track with assured status, income and pension. However for the students in this study to remain in pursuit of the economic model of adulthood meant identity crisis at an existential level, in terms of what meaning they sought to impose on their lives. Although they would appear to have more choice, than say the offenders in Laverick's chapter (chapter six); the students' perceptions were that socio-economic trends were forcing them to 'opt out' and seek alternative identity and meaning sources. The risky strategies taken by the students involved long-term independent travelling; doing unpaid or low paid charity/voluntary work; seeking out parenthood; and reverting to traditional religious identities. All of these are very contrastive strategies but all carry risks to the long-term identity and status of the individuals in relation to dominant economic and cultural discourses. As Scott Jones notes, the students acknowledge that their ways of dealing with 'deferred' adulthood are temporary and represent 'delaying' tactics rather than alternative ways of being. Just as Laverick's offenders in chapter six must be brought to account for their violence, and Watt's civil servants in chapter seven must 'get with the programme', then these young adults will eventually have to 'risk' participation in the 'proper' adult world. This echoes Foucault's (1990, 1991, and 2003) contention that 'resistances' are only temporary and are contingent to changing contexts and discourses.

Risky Meanings

What is significant in this volume are the ways in which risks are associated, harness and frame life trajectories of 'be-coming' desired identity locations or identity-attributes. For example Dave Merryweather's work (chapter five) critically maps out the discursive and affective investments young men place in a desired masculinity, while Laverick's (chapter six) moving piece charts 'be-coming' 'hard' to survive the normative requirements of a specific community. Similarly, Raisborough's (chapter two) argument details the normative requirements of authentic femininity that motivate certain risk practices, in this case, undergoing elective cosmetic surgery. It is hardly surprising that in almost all of the chapters authenticity was a component part of identity construction, whether in being a 'real athlete, man, worker, or mother. As identities become more fluid within late Modernity (Giddens 1991) it is to be expected that a search for the 'really real' or authentic would become an aspect of a wider meaning search (Berger 1974)

All of the case studies explore identities as they are lived in specific social and cultural contexts and the 'choices' around risk are rationalised, perceived and acted upon. In doing so the issue of 'what is normal' is raised in relation to, among other things, body shape, violence and pregnancy. Normalcy is mediated by and through 'expert' and institutional sources of knowledge; discourses of gender, sexuality, class and age; and lived experiences. The degree of agency, choice and resistance that individuals have in the face of normalising discourses is contingent on socio-cultural context. At the heart of all this risky business of negotiation, discourse, agency and self-actualisation is a search for meaning.

Late modernity is characterised as a time of potential 'meaning crisis' (Weber 1990; Berger 1974; Giddens 1990; Bauman 2001) as Modernity's certainties, traditions and securities fall away. The individual was once attached to a series of communal and social solidarities and identities, which provided status and helped the individual to impose meaning on the social world. In doing this, the individual achieved some degree of ontological security. However, late modernity ushers in an era where ontological security is increasingly elusive and thus risk discourses emerge. As ontological security declines, then individuals are forced to seek out ways to construct meanings that are increasingly reliant on the self as a source of meaning. Therefore the search for meaning, which Weber (1990), identifies as an intrinsic aspect of social groups, becomes embedded in the processes of identity construction and self actualisation. More research needs to be done that further explores the links between risk discourses, meaning search and identity.

References

Adams, M. (2003), 'The Reflexive Self and Culture: A Critique', *British Journal of Sociology* 54:2, 221–38.
Bauman, Z. (1992), *Intimations of Postmodernity* (London: Routledge).
—— (2001), *The Individualised Society* (Cambridge: Polity Press).
Beck, U. (1992), *Risk Society: Towards A New Modernity* (London: Sage).
—— et al. (1994), *Reflexive Modernisation: Politics, Tradition and Aesthetics in the Modern Social Order* (Cambridge: Polity).
—— (2000), *The Brave New World of Work* (Cambridge: Polity Press).

Bennett, T. and Watson, D. (eds) (2002), *Understanding Everyday Life* (Oxford: Blackwell).

Berger, P. L. and Luckmann, T. (1967), *The Social Construction of Reality: A Treatise in the Sociology of Knowledge* (London: Allen Lane).

Berger, P. L. et al. (1974), *The Homeless Mind: Modernization and Consciousness* (London: Pelican Books).

Berger, P. L. (1991), *Invitation to Sociology* (Harmondsworth: Penguin).

Brannen, J. and Nilsen, A. (2005), 'Individualisation, Choice and Structure: A Discussion of Current Trends in Sociological Analysis', *The Sociological Review* 53:3, 412–28.

Charon, J. M. (ed.) (2004), *Symbolic Interactionism: An Introduction, An Interpretation, An Integration* (Upper Saddle River, JJ: Pearson Prentice Hall).

Cuff, E. C. et al. (2006), *Perspectives in Sociology* (London: Routledge).

Davies, K. (1995), *Reshaping the Female Body: The Dilemma of Cosmetic Surgery* (London: Routledge).

Denzin, N. K. (1989), *Interpretive Interactionism* (Newbury Park, CA: London).

Denzin, N. K. and Lincoln, Y. S. (eds) (2000), *The Handbook of Qualitative Research* (London: Sage).

Douglas, M. (1978), *Purity and Danger: An Analysis of Concepts of Pollution and Taboo* (London: Routledge and Kegan Paul).

—— (1994), *Risk and Blame: Essays in Cultural Theory* (London: Routledge).

Epstein, D. and Steinberg, D. L. (1998), 'American Dreamin': Discoursing Liberally on the Oprah Winfrey Show', *Women's Studies International Forum* 21:1, 77–94.

Evans, M. (2003), *Gender and Social Theory* (Buckingham: Open University Press).

Foucault, M. (1989), *The Order of Things* (London: Routledge).

—— (1990), *The History of Sexuality Vol 1. An Introduction* (New York, NY: Vintage).

—— (1991), *Discipline and Punish* (London: Penguin).

—— (2003), *The Birth of the Clinic* (London: Routledge).

Friedan, B. (1963), *The Feminine Mystique* (New York, NY: Gollancz).

Furedi, F (2004), *Therapy Culture: Cultivating Vulnerability in an Uncertain Age* (London: Routledge).

Gardiner, M. (2000), *Critiques of Everyday Life* (London: Routledge).

Giddens, A. (1990), *The Consequences of Modernity* (Cambridge: Polity).

—— (1991), *Modernity and Self Identity: Self and Society in a Late Modern Age* (Cambridge: Polity).

Goffman, E. (1959), *The Presentation of Self in Everyday Life* (New York, NY: Doubleday).

Green, E. and Singleton, C. (2006), 'Risky bodies at leisure: young women negotiating time and place', *Sociology* 40 (5): 853–71.

Hall, S. (1992), 'The Question of Cultural Identity' in Hall, S. et al. (eds) (1992), *Modernity and its Futures* (Cambridge: Polity Press).

Highmore, B. (2002), *Everyday Life and Cultural Theory: An Introduction* (London: Routledge).

Jeffreys, S. (2005), *Beauty and Misogyny: Harmful Cultural Practices in the West* (London: Routledge).

Layder, D. (1994), *Understanding Social Theory* (London: Sage).

Layder, D. (1997), *Modern Social Theory: Key Debates and New Directions* (London: UCL Press).

Lupton, D. and Tulloch, J. (2001), 'Border Crossings: Narratives of Movement, 'Home' and 'Risk', *Sociological Research Online* 5:4. <http://www.socresonline.org.uk/5/4/lupton.html>

—— (2002), 'Life Would Be Pretty Dull Without Risk: Voluntary Risk-Taking and Its Pleasures', *Health, Risk and Society* 4:2, 113–24.

Lyotard, J. (1984), *The Postmodern Condition: A Report on Knowledge* (Manchester: Manchester University Press).

McNay, L. (2000), *Gender and Agency* (Cambridge: Polity Press).

Nevin, L. (2006), The Third Leader; Skin Deep: *The Independent* 13 July.

Palmer, S (2006), *Toxic Childhood* (London: Orion).

Pitts, V. (2003), *In The Flesh: The Cultural Politics of Body Modification* (Basingstoke: Palgrave).

Ramazanoglu, C. (ed.) (1993), *Up Against Foucault: Explorations of Some Tensions between Foucault and Feminism* (London: Routledge).

Rich, A. (1979), *On Lies, Secrets and Silence: Selected Prose 1966–1978* (New York, NY: W.W. Norton).

Ritzer, G. (1992), *Contemporary Sociological Theory* (London: McGraw-Hill).

Rose, N. (1999), *Governing the Soul: The Shaping of the Private Self* (London: Free Association Books).

Stanley, L. (1988), 'Historical sources for studying work and leisure in women's lives', in E. Wimbush and M. Talbot (eds) (1988), *Relative Freedoms: Woman and Leisure* (Buckingham: Open University Press).

Tulloch, J. and Lupton, D. (2003), *Risk and Everyday Life* (London: Sage).

Weber, M. (1990), *From Max Weber: Essays in Sociology* (edited by Gerth, H. H. and Wright Mills, C.), (London: Routledge and Kegan Paul).

Wright Mills, C. W. (1970), *The Sociological Imagination* (Harmondsworth: Penguin).

Chapter 2

Contexts of Choice: The Risky Business of Elective Cosmetic Surgery

Jayne Raisborough

Little attention is paid to why patients are willing to take the risk of having cosmetic surgery (Davies 1995, 38).

The production of self as a visual display, as a fit slim, young-looking and fashionably adorned body, does not represent a range of choices but a single imperative of the consumer capitalist context of contemporary existence (Frost 2005, 69).

Introduction

The emergence of Foucauldian-influenced poststructuralism in sociological theories of risk has enabled attention onto the micro-politics of the everyday and on the ways individuals make sense of, relate to and take up risk. This has gone some way to curb the enthusiasm of prevailing claims that the self in late modernity, whilst busy foraging a detraditionalised socio-economic landscape to construct its biography, is reflexively, rationally risk aversive; anxiously seeking to avoid or minimise risks (Giddens 1991; Beck 1992). That curbing is thought necessary, is evident in the increasing concern that conceptualisations of a restless and risk-phobic self tend to deny the socio-cultural contexts that give 'self', 'risk' and 'reflexivity' meaning, expression and opportunity (McNay 2000; Adams 2003; Bradden and Nilsen 2005). Locating risk in the unfolding of everyday life can thus be considered a deft move to re-contextualise the self and biography construction by realising the often complex relations that individuals might have with risk.

Key to a project of re-contextualisation is Deborah Lupton and John Tulloch's identification of the 'voluntary risk-taker' (2002): defined as one who recognises risks but from choice faces them often for the purpose of self-development. While there is greater analytical purchase afforded by moving away from assumptions of risk-avoidance, this chapter question whether 'choice', itself often conceptually bounded with liberal notions of autonomy and empowerment (Epstein and Steinberg 1998; Jeffreys 2005), weakens our ability to firmly embed risks within their socio-cultural contexts. By extending Lupton and Tulloch's (2002) recognition that active risk-uptake may function as specific 'practices of the self',[1] this chapter maps out the moral contexts in which choices associated with elective cosmetic surgery are recognised and realised. In so doing, it argues for closer critical attention to the dynamics of gender relations upon risk-decisions as a means to more adequately grasp the uses, meanings and choices surrounding risk in the everyday realities of those who experience them.

Cosmetic Surgery

Cosmetic surgery generally refers to an increasing range of medical interventions aimed at improving or modifying the appearance of the body (Haiken 1997). While it is by no means a recent phenomena, its history can be dated to at least 600 BC as demonstrated in Hindu surgeons' descriptions of nose reconstructions (Haiken 1997), the sheer scale of its technological advancements (such as out-patient laser surgery) allows it unparalleled intervention into the look and function of the contemporary body. As 'nose jobs', 'boob jobs' and wrinkle-reductions become more commonplace (Hall 2007), the body can be moulded by liposuction; blepharoplasty (eye-lid surgery); chemical peels; 'tummy tucks'; bone reconfiguration; radical dentistry; amputation; implants; sub-incision (splitting of the penis); and skin-bleaching (Davies 2003; Pitts 2003; Ashikari 2005; Hall 2007): the publicity surrounding labiaplasty (the so-called 'designer vagina') suggests that there is little which cannot be tucked or trimmed (Navarro 2004).

No longer solely reserved for celebrities or the wealthy (Sarwer 2002), Britons spent over £600 million on surgery in 2006 (Nevin 2006) and this is a market that is likely to see sharp growth as private surgeries deploy the marketing practices of supermarkets such as loyalty cards (5 per cent off future procedures), holiday vouchers and payment plans (Hall 2006). While there are a growing number of men engaging with cosmetic surgery (Gill et al. 2005; Jeffreys 2005), and leaving aside the figures for the circumcision of American infant boys (see Harrison 2002), it is estimated that 90 per cent of Western consumers of cosmetic surgery are women (Davies 1995; Haiken 1997; Davies 2002; Hall 2007). It has been reported that most British women expect to have some form of surgery in their life time: the most common being face-lifts and breast enhancement (Hall 2006). This expectation in itself indicates the increasing normalisation of cosmetic surgery (Banet-Weiser and Portwood-Stacer 2006), evidenced in part, by the way that material once deemed suitable for the advertisement sections in women's 'glossy' magazines now commands the attention in grabbing headlines, problem-pages, and full length features.

However, cosmetic surgery is risky. Risk is normally associated with cosmetic surgery in terms of surgical mishaps or the faulty practices of unscrupulous or

---

1 See Merryweather in this volume for a further discussion of Foucault's practices of the self in relation to performances of desired masculinity.

untrained surgeons (Davies 1995; Mills 2002). Stories of infection; scarring; multiple 'corrective' surgeries; encapsulation and rejection of implants; toxic reactions; embolisms; blindness; 'roaming' implants; disfigurement; loss of sensation/control; shock; disappointment; and death as a result of surgery 'gone wrong' (Morgan 1991; Davies 1995; Hall 2001; Mills 2002; Jeffreys 2005) are widely published and avidly consumed by a societal audience already literate in the 'horrors' of elective surgery. Yet, as the body emerges as a key site for identity construction in late modernity, whereby 'we are responsible for the design of our bodies' (Giddens 1991, 102), more people elect to engage with these risks,[2] or plan to, and this suggests that Lupton and Tulloch's (2002) notion of voluntary risk-taking is an appropriate start to generate explanations as to why cosmetic surgery enjoys an increasing customer base despite its well publicised 'horrors'.

The Voluntary Risk-taker

Departing from prevailing conceptualisations of risk-avoidance, Lupton and Tulloch (2001; 2002) apply a poststructuralist framework to focus on the meanings individuals impute to risks as they are realised in the routines of their everyday lives; as such their work is key to a project of re-contextualisation whereby 'risk', 'self' and the processes of biography construction are understood as both emerging from, and embedded within, specific socio-cultural contexts. By critically teasing out the discursive strategies through which risk is understood by the individuals in their sample, Lupton and Tulloch (2002) recognise that risks may be actively pursued as part of an individual's biography construction. Their identification of the 'voluntary risk taker' speaks not only to those who actively engage in risky activities, such as extreme sports, but also to individuals who are aware that their activities and decisions are 'in some sense risky' but proceed nonetheless 'deliberately and from choice' (Lupton and Tulloch 2002, 115).

Within personal stories of risks involved in surfing; riding rodeo; immigration; going into a new business venture; taking out a mortgage; and revealing sexual identity, Lupton and Tulloch (2002) identified discourses relating to the excitement and thrills of risk-taking and to the role of risk in motivating self-improvement and the realisation of an authentic self. Their research suggested that while risks may be enjoyed for the pleasure of facing and overcoming fear, or testing one's physical and mental capabilities under stress, some individuals perceived the taking of risks to be vital in moving them from a present state of inertia (or comfort zone) to one of self-determined action, self-actualisation and progress. Lupton and Tulloch (2002)

---

2 The British Association of Aesthetic Plastic Surgeons reported a 90 per cent increase in the number of liposuction operations in 2006 compared to 2005. In the same period the demand for face lifts increased by 44 per cent; eyelid surgery by 48 per cent and brow lifts 50 per cent. 92 per cent of operations in 2006 were carried out on women (Hall 2007).

concluded that active and voluntary engagement with perceived risks functioned as particular 'practices of the self' (Foucault 1988), permitting the development and expression of subjectivity in relation to late modernity's preoccupation with self-work: as Giddens notes, in late modernity 'we are not what we are, but what we make of ourselves' (1991, 68) and this sentiment is echoed through the narratives of those who use risks to 'make something of themselves'.

On the face of it, the motivation to 'make something of themselves' serves as an initial explanation for why some may face the risks of elective cosmetic surgery. Yet, a Foucauldian-influenced poststructuralism demands greater attention to the operations and processes through which risks are understood and relatedly how cosmetic surgery takes hold on the cultural imaginary as a possible and legitimate means to 'make something' of ones' self. Hazeldean (2003, 415) argues that poststructuralism can 'aid social thought in grasping certain present realities of how things work', and it is the question of how everyday present realities incite an individual to engage with the risks of cosmetic surgery that is the major focus of this chapter. In this sense Lupton and Tulloch's (2002) identification of the voluntary risk-taker provides a useful entry point into the elective nature of cosmetic surgery. However, 'making something' of one's self does little to explain why it is women who are currently overrepresented in the numbers of people undergoing cosmetic surgery. It is here that a gender analysis is required.

Gender and Risk

Although 'gender' cannot be equated solely with 'woman', women's location within an existing (and persisting) engendered social order does still warrant close scrutiny and the application of gender analysis, that is to say that a focus on the discursive and material conditions of women's lives is still a political necessity (Scraton 1994; Gordon et al. 2005; Raisborough 2006). However, Lupton and Tulloch's work (2001; 2002), while observing gender differences, hesitates to apply a gender analysis as a means to critically explore the ways that gender relations shape the political and material contexts of everyday lives and choices made therein. This is despite their awareness that restrictions enforced by normative gender relations encouraged one of their interviewees to seek out risks that allowed her to disrupt conventions of femininity: 'Being a girl, you have to take risks by trying to overcome the taboos that [limit] women' Lorraine cited in Lupton and Tulloch (2002,118). In addition, they give relatively little analytical space to their realisation that gender relations operate in the ways that men and women perceive and define risk. While the men in their sample described risks in terms of sport, travel and 'daring deeds' (2002, 327), women were more likely to locate risk in terms of sexual practice (unwanted or unsafe sex and pregnancy) and violence. This suggests that gender could offer critical purchase on the political contexts that position women as culpable if they 'attract' unwanted sexual attention and which further operates to reproduce the sexual double standard which directs and shapes that attention (Patton and Mannison 1998; Jackson and Cram 2003). More widely it suggests that women's location in a gendered social order, which may be differentially experienced (Gordon et al. 2005), not only shapes their perception and definition of risk but may also prompt specific risk choices. Recent empirical work for example, has demonstrated that cultural notions of 'respectability' and a generalised sense of male violence both shape women's risk perceptions; their mobility (viewing the home as a safe space) and their risk-behaviours (Green and Singleton 2006).

The Matter of Choice

Critical attention to the dynamics of gender and risk may be crowded out by the emphasis upon choice in Lupton and Tulloch's (2002) definition of a voluntary risk-taker. Defining the risk-taker as one proceeding deliberately and from choice is useful, as Lupton and Tulloch (2002) argue, in isolating those risk activities which may be viewed by a wider culture as 'risky' but not so by subcultures or individuals who engage in them, and those risks which individuals cannot avoid or may be unaware of. Yet, there is some concern that the highly individualised discourses that accompany 'choice' can serve to conceptually isolate the individual from their (engendered) contextual relations (Gill et al. 2005). Brannen and Nilsen (2005) argue that concepts of choice are saturated with neo-liberal Western ideals of individual freedom and autonomous agency to such an extent that any analysis of the contexts and material conditions in which choices are offered and made, finds little critical space both within social science analysis and in the ways individuals speak and think of their everyday lives. As an example of the latter, Epstein and Steinberg (1998) analysed the ways individuals spoke of their choices on the American talk-show, *The Oprah Winfrey Show.* They observed a celebrated reification of choice, stressing however, that it was the *exercise* of choice which received audience approval. They concluded that

> In this context, the kinds of choices individuals made and the conditions of choosing became eclipsed by the fact that choices *were* made: choice itself seemed to be taken as a testament to freedom, democracy, and the American Way and ... therefore, unquestionable (1998, 93).

McNay (2000) draws critical attention to these 'conditions of choosing' by arguing that gender relations and inequalities endure and are re-made through the changes marking late modernity. For McNay (2000) gender has a present and historical political reality that has not been erased and cannot be easily shrugged off through expressions of personal, reflexive agency and choice. Such is the disjuncture between engendered material realities and discourses of individualised free choice, that Gordon et al. (2005) argue that women daily live out a tensile contradiction posed by being a 'woman' and being an 'individual' in the face of choice. Yet, the individualised narratives of choice mask these lived experiences by conceptually dislocating individuals from their wider political contexts (Galvin 2002; Jeffreys 2005). For Brannen and Nilsen (2005) the consequence is that gender (and class) start to lose their analytic potential and are regulated to individual attributes or variables in risk choices. It is this chapter's contention that it is only through mapping out individual choices in relation to wider contextual relations, in this case engendered realities, that a nuanced and meaningful understanding of risk in the everyday can be realised.

There is, however, an opportunity for a tighter re-contextualisation of risk-choices within these material realities offered by Foucault's (1988) 'practices of the self', which Lupton and Tulloch (2002) concluded but did not have the space to explore. This opportunity is suggested in Foucault's (1987) emphasis that the promotion and possibilities of self-refashioning rest not in the individual, but in the contextual relations in which the individual is situated:

> There practices are ... not something that the individual invents by himself. They are patterns that he finds in his culture and which are proposed, suggested, imposed on him by his culture, his society and his social group (Foucault 1987, 122).

While Foucault's later work lacks development and has been roundly criticised for its neglect of gender relations (Ramazanoglu 1993; Smart 1998), others have defended his work against the criticism that he failed to provide an emancipatory theory and related practices (Weedon 1997; Sawicki 1998). Sawicki (1998, 105) for example, argues that Foucault's contribution is as a provider of *tools* 'that subjugated individuals may enlist in a particular set of struggles' to question the possibilities of the present. In terms of this chapter's intentions, these tools and questions offer a way to broaden out individual choices to wider contextual relations and 'conditions of choosing'. More specifically, Foucault's attention to the possibilities of the present alert us to the operations of the moral economy which as outlined in the next section, shapes the context in which much of our choosing and refashioning takes place.

Incitement to Self-manage: Risk and Morality

Foucault's (1988) 'practices of self' forms part of his later work, which is generally characterised by an attempt to temper his overarching focus on relations of domination and subjection by exploring the plays of productive power (Moss 1998; McNay 2000). Foucault's notion of 'governance', defined as the 'conduct of conduct' (1982, 220–1), relates to ways of 'acting on ourselves, so that the police, the guards and the doctors do not have to' (Cruikshank 1993, 300). It refers to two related aspects; the ways that a modern ethos on 'management' (of things and of self) emerges and takes hold and, the ways in which individuals are recruited into productive power relations through self-care, self-management and self-surveillance (Moss 1998). For Foucault the body becomes a key site for governance. He argues that modern rationality promotes increased body-awareness through various discursive strategies which seduce individuals into their own self-management (Foucault 1986). Individuals are recruited into improving, maintaining and *managing* their own body projects as an available means to 'cultivate the self' (Foucault 1986, 39); that is to comply with the temporally and culturally specific moral and ethical frameworks of being (Galvin 2002). 'Cultivation' involves opening the self and body to expert interrogation and intervention as expert knowledge systems become the legitimate optic through which the body and self, and their work/ projects become intelligible. 'Practices of the self' and the choices one makes as part of creating oneself are therefore necessarily located and made possible through wider relations of productive power – as such, this offers a useful lens through which to more sharply contextualise the choices surrounding cosmetic surgery.

Risk plays an important function here; as others have noted that the individual is motivated into choices relating to self-management through discursive constructions of the body as 'at risk' (Petersen 1997; Galvin 2002). This is particularly evident in health discourses where 'risk' serves to expand notions of illness, disease and body-failure from the ill to all. As the body is constructed as always vulnerable to its own internal corruptions or the exposure to external threats of infection and accident; risk-reduction and risk-avoidance are marketed through health promotion as helping to empower 'active patients' to choose self-care, risk reducing management regimes (Fitzpatrick 2000). What is particularly pertinent here is the operation of a powerful moral impulse; as risks are closely aligned with lifestyle *choices* (high fat diet, unsafe sex and so on) risk-avoidance becomes a moral enterprise (Galvin 2002; Hallowell and Lawton 2002). To clarify, Rosin (1997, 380) states that 'something is in the moral domain if the term *ought* (or *ought not*) applies to it'; and there are observable means by which choices are brought into the moral domain; both through 'expert' constructions of the 'healthy' body as the ethical substance for self-work, and in the recent spate of television programmes clearly outlining what one 'ought' or 'ought not' to wear, eat, clean and do.[3] The discursive relations between morality and lifestyle choices have powerful repercussions on the recognition of an individual's citizenship and personhood as what one 'ought' to do reflects one's moral capital in a socio-economic landscape marked by the retreat of the welfare state (Galvin 2002; Lawler 2005). Gill et al. (2005, 55) are clear that the individualised discourses that promote responsible body work also render individuals as 'morally culpable if they

---

3 Such television programmes include the BBC's *What Not To Wear* and *Honey, We're Killing the Kids* and Channel Four's *How Clean is your House?* and *You are What you Eat.* These tend to follow a set formula; to identify a problem with the participant's life; use of shock tactics to encourage a participant to acknowledge their problem and often, its damage to the self, family and friends; to solve the problem in the space of the programme through expert intervention, the application of rules, education and extensive surveillance; and finally to demonstrate the success of expert intervention in the 'reveal' (see Epstein and Steinberg (1997) and McRobbie (2004) for related discussions).

fail'.[4] What is significant here for our discussion of cosmetic surgery is that it is not just the 'unhealthy body' but the 'unattractive body' that stands a marker of 'moral failure' (Gill et al. 2005; Banet-Weiser and Portwood-Stacer 2006).

Additionally, the moral impulse operating within those mechanisms termed by Foucault as 'practices of the self', rests not only on the health of the external body, but also requires careful attention to the health of the inner self. The growth of 'therapy culture' (Furedi 2004), cultivated by the increasing legitimacy of what Rose (1999) calls 'psy' discourses (psychotherapy, psychoanalysis and psychology more generally) help construct notions of a self in a possible risky relationship with its 'inner', 'authentic' self. The persisting, albeit uneven, engendered discursive constructions of women as the emotional labourers for both the self and the family operate to position women as targets for such self-help work (Epstein and Steinberg 1998). Hazeldean's (2003) analysis of self-help books, by way of an example, critically charts the ways in which discursive strategies posit a relationship between the 'self' and the 'inner self' that is potentially risky if neglected or lost. The authentic self can be misplaced by the pressures of everyday life; the demanding impositions of others; and losing sight of one's dreams and aspirations within the dull cushioning of mundane routines. Self-work that repairs the breach becomes an ethical project of autonomy, responsibility and control, and marks an 'effective, well adjusted individual in charge of her emotional life' (2003, 424). The self is therefore, following Hazeldean (2003), 'risky', either from its divorce from authenticity or from insufficient duty to, and vigilance of, its true and inner needs. Yet self-work is also dragged into the moral domain; far from being selfish, the work towards a responsible, autonomous selfhood is itself social obligation: Self-work, then,

> permits and requires a notion of social obligation in that technologies of the self such as self-discipline and self knowledge are the 'right' or ethical thing to take on, no only for the sake of the self, but for one's partner and for wider society (Hazeldean 2003, 42).

What emerges from this discussion so far is that governance involves not only risk-reduction body programmes but also a visible demonstration of physical and mental well-being as a means to claim citizenship in the moral economy. Some of this is suggested in Lupton and Tulloch's (2002) conclusion that risk uptake can feature as Foucault's (1988) 'practices of the self', but wider space is opened up by unpacking Foucault's (1988) stress on wider patterns and on the operations of morality therein.

This space could be used to explore the manifestation and shape of specific risks as they materialise in the cultural imaginary as possible and acceptable vehicles for self-work. This involves asking how cosmetic surgery, with its attendant risks, presents an intelligible choice for women. It is clear from Lupton and Tulloch's

---

4 The unfolding moral panic developing around the 'threat' of obesity offers an illuminating example (see Gard and Wright 2005).

(2002) sample that certain risks (for example, a business venture or taking out a mortgage) could be considered more 'acceptable' and socially intelligible because they are risks that signal maturity, growth and progression. There may be many ways that women can leave a 'comfort zone', but those valued may be those which speak to lauded neo-liberal values of responsibility and autonomy. There is then, arguably, both an emergence and shaping of risks in terms of their 'fit for purpose'. To suggest as much alerts critical attention to question what forms of risk emerge, which ones are recognised and by whom, and then taken-up for self-work. These questions go some way to contextualise choice.

Contextualising Surgery as an Intelligible Risk-choice for Women

In a recent analysis of television reality shows that 'make-over' their participants, Banet-Weiser and Portwood-Stacer (2006, 256) concluded that such media exposure was both reflective and constitutive of the 'increasing normalisation of the cultural practice of cosmetic surgery'. It is this 'increasing normalisation' that helps bring into focus the context in which women approach and realise their risk-choices. What is of concern in this section is the processes through which cosmetic surgery becomes a culturally intelligible, normalised and appropriate technology, a focus which in turn, opens some space to explore the functions 'risk' might play in those processes.

So far this chapter has argued that the body has an unprecedented centrality to 'the modern person's sense of self identity' (Shilling 1993, 3), and it has suggested that it is the physical appearance and image of that body that signals one's moral worth (McRobbie 2004). This clearly entices both men and women into a relationship of biography construction, choice, 'moral' body-work and consumer capitalism (Galvin 2002; Frost 2005). Yet, although men's bodies are increasingly commodifed (Gill et al. 2005), it is women's bodies that are additionally objectified and fetishised in a gendered order that has long judged women's worth in terms of their bodily appearance (Millsted and Frith 2003) Feminist research has critically charted the ways in which women's 'excessive' bodies, hair and 'looks' are associated with immorality, unrespectability and significantly, unfemininity (see Jeffreys 2005). Such work argues that the heightened and unflinching cultural visibility of women's bodies affords many women little option but to perform gendered identities based on appearance (Frost 2005). There is, of course, following Foucault, room for resistance, but stepping outside the normative ('letting oneself go') carries such consequences that Skeggs (1997, 100) argues many women have to negotiate hegemonic beauty norms to avoid being positioned as 'vulgar, pathological, tasteless and sexual', and as McRobbie (2004) adds, dishonest and unemployable. If, as Jeffreys (2005) argues, elective surgery can be regarded, and is certainly marketed, as a logical extension to women's daily beauty regimes then the risks faced are not only culturally intelligible but are afforded a degree of normalisation[5] as part of women's 'doing' respectable femininity in the everyday.

Yet, the discursive-material relationship between appearance and femininity can be further understood by approaching the intelligibility of risk-taking in terms of the moral self-work discussed above. Such explication helps to map out the 'doing' of femininity onto the 'doing' of neo-liberal citizenship that comes from prevailing 'practices of the self' grounded in responsibility and biography expression. Negrin's (2000, 86) observation that 'individual physical appearance is taken to be the mirror of the soul' offers a useful starting point. If moral self-worth is tied to the 'mirroring' of the authentic inner onto the external body, then surgical intervention to modify the external body takes further hold on the cultural imaginary as a credible and legitimate means of self-work and the expression of worth.

Ashby (2000) is clear that despite poststructuralist disputes on the status of the unified self, cosmetic surgery presents the consumer with the ability to rescue a body by shaping its contours in such ways that fully express the life, energy and desires of an identifiable, coherent and authentic inner: 'the assumption underlying this is that our internal self is our 'true' self, that the body or outer self, does not reflect' (Ashby 2000, 46). For example, Gagnè and McGaughey's (2002, 821) research on women choosing to undergo surgical breast enhancement found that some were motivated by their belief that 'their breasts belied the self within the body'. Truth operates powerfully here; in the past cosmetics and adornment have been regarded as tools for women's inherent duplicity (Negrin 2000), now, the creation of an inner self as the substance for self-work affords cosmetic surgery a moral legitimacy as a means to express the truth and authenticity that rests within. As Gagnè and McGaughey conclude, cosmetic surgery emerges in late modernity as a legitimate technology of 'feminization' (2002, 819) through which women display their authentic, embodied, feminine self.

However, this strongly suggests the production of *specific* forms of authentic femininity. Feminist research has critically observed how hegemonic ideals of beauty guide the surgeon's knife (Haiken 1997; Davies 2003; Ashikari 2005),[6] but there may be something else to say about the production of authentic femininity as cosmetic surgery increasingly manifests as a credible vehicle for personal transformation in late modernity. This function of cosmetic surgery constitutes the specific focus of reality television, which clearly stresses that it is not only bodies but *lives* that are 'made over' (Banet-Weiser and Portwood-Stacer 2006):

---

5 Everyday beauty regimes are themselves painful and risky. Jeffreys (2005) details the pain involved in waxing, plucking, corset-wearing and in the wearing of high-heeled shoes. She also details the health risks carried by the daily absorption of the carcinogenic cocktails within make-up and hair-dye.

6 The main argument is that cosmetic surgeons work to ideals of proportion and symmetry that are grounded in a white western aesthetic of female beauty. Ashikari (2005) adds that notions of national identity and appearance also shape aesthetic ideals.

The new bodies do not have just bigger breasts, more pronounced cheekbones, and whiter teeth. Rather, the programs [sic] suggest that individuals undergoing multiple cosmetic surgery procedures become livelier, more outgoing, and psychologically contented individuals. Personal growth or spiritual development used to be connected to taking a pilgrimage to Thailand, watching Oprah, or training for marathon runs. Now, apparently, you need buttock implants or breast augmentation to let your true authentic self emerge (Turner 2005 cited in Banet-Weiser and Portwood-Stacer 2006, 265).

That personal life transformation and growth accompanies the attainment of a surgically modified body, or body part, could be understood, following feminist research, as a product of achieving (some) embodied stake in hegemonic beauty norms - that is to 'be' or to pass as beautiful (Gagnè and McGaughey 2002), yet the emphasis on personal transformation also makes explicit the self-work and necessary consumption required by and for the authentic self that is prompted by neo-liberal governance. Banet-Weiser and Portwood-Stacer (2006) draw out the significance here to argue that ideal femininity is discursively mingled with constructions of neo-liberal citizenship. To clarify, Galvin (2002, 108) defines the good citizen 'as someone who actively participates in social and economic life, makes rational choices and is independent, self-reliant and responsible'. This definition necessarily invokes an active, healthy and importantly, flexible body able to keep pace with the demands of a fast-changing market economy (Katz 2000; McRobbie 2004). In her observation of neo-liberal western democracies Galvin (2002) notes a revival of classic notions of negative liberty, which posit the displacement of state responsibility onto citizens' empowered and informed choices. In this light, choices around the production of a healthy, transformed, authentic self and body are reshaped as one's individual responsibility to seek market-placed resources for meaningful biography construction and to signal viability in the market-economy. Choice, then, is not only an effect of that displacement but also the lived instances through which the autonomous exercise of choice is a key marker of citizenship; it is the moment of establishing a claim of citizenry and being recognised as a viable citizen through that claim. It could follow that the 'choice' of cosmetic surgery has a performative function as the expression of self-actualised, autonomous, ethical self-worth and the exercise of women's empowered citizenry as consumers. As such, cosmetic surgery may be, as Banet-Weiser and Portwood-Stacer argue, 'the ultimate expression of individual transformation and a kind of empowerment' (2006, 261).

That this is the case is sharply indicated in the ways that women's choice to transform the body is constructed, marketed, recognised and experienced as an empowered declaration of neo-liberal citizenship and 'respectable' femininity. Indeed, as appearance and the engagement with self-work become more normalised as ways of 'doing' identity and citizenship, the vehicles of transformation – surgery – increase their own intelligibility as normalised and available resources. The role and function of risk is discussed below but it is worth suggesting here that, if this can be said about cosmetic surgery, then the 'risks' lie not just in the clinical technicalities and medical mishaps but also in the consequence to women's stake in citizenry based on moral worth if they choose *not* to engage with this increasing normalised vehicle of personal transformation.

The Function of Risk

That said there *are* risks and pain involved in surgery. Elective surgery is a gamble and carries many risks of severe and permanent pain, suffering and discomfort (Davies 1995; Jeffreys 2005; Hall 2007). While the long-list of medical risks may be regarded as possible disincentives to opt to go 'under the knife' this section explores whether well-publicised risks serve a particular function in the legitimacy of cosmetic surgery as vehicle of self-work.

In order for cosmetic surgery to present as a credible means for personal transformation it needs to distance itself from associations of vanity and narcissism. Hazeldean (2003) makes this useful point in relation to self-help literature arguing that such distancing is made possible through the presentation of personal transformation as a journey that is unavoidably risky and painful. This presentation helps market the seriousness of the journey towards self-actualisation (it is not to be undertaken lightly), and provides a site for individuals to measure and test their own commitment in relation to how they face those risks. Risks function as difficult challenges, with the not so subtle suggestion that any failure to transform rests in the inability of the individual to overcome them (see also Epstein and Steinberg 1998). While there may be differences between the risks in self-help literature, which are those posed by the thwarting powers of the old self refusing to let the authentic self emerge, and the consequences should surgery go wrong, there is some purchase in viewing risks as a necessary construction of the material and emotional process of transformation.

This is indicated in Banet-Weiser and Portwood-Stacer's (2006) analysis of 'make-over' shows which give a good deal of air time to uncompromising details of the surgery itself in comparison to the 'reveal'; the point at which the results of the surgery can be seen. They argue that this increases the cultural visibility of the *process* of transformation and by virtue of its difficulty, the effort and determination of those undergoing it:

> The physical evidence of transformation, along with what appear to be the unadulterated expression of pain by the subjects provide unequivocal proof that change has taken place and leave no room for doubt that the procedures depicted have resulted in a beautiful body (Banet-Weiser and Portwood-Stacer 2006, 265).

The favouring of process over product is important, they argue, in adding the authenticity of the 'freeing' from 'earlier lives' (2006, 263), proving that change has taken place and that transformation is possible. Gill et al. (2005) offer further support, claiming that the details of process-related pain helps distance surgery from accusations of vanity; that one is willing to undergo such suffering with no set guarantee of desired results, adds a certain moral legitimacy to an individual's commitment. Indeed, they argue that such constructions are important in developing a male consumer base. However, what is understated in both these accounts is the way in which publicised risks help to highlight and keep to the fore the difficulties and challenges of the process and in so doing help maintain cosmetic surgery as a legitimate enterprise. By articulating what could 'go wrong', risks are discursively deployed to amplify the challenges an individual must face. As such, risks play an important function in framing the process of transformation in ways that emphasise commitment to self-work and in adding authenticity to it. Authenticity here relates not only to the constructions of an authentic self which demands risks are taken, thus neatly suturing agency exercised in the site of surgery to the performative practices of the moral economy, but it also suggests a reality of the process itself, which cosmetic surgery can quite visibly demonstrate and literally mark on the body.

It remains to add that risk may serve a further function by creating a site of articulation of consumer choices for some women. That is to say that it is in the evaluation and 'facing' of risks that rational, reflexive autonomy is performed through choice-decisions. As risks of surgery are increasingly known, choices to continue may be articulated through declarations that risks are 'worth' taking for the perceived material and symbolic benefits that a viable feminine body secures (albeit temporarily). In short, those risks are worth facing if the self has worth.[7] In addition, the evaluative articulations which follow from known risks enable women to take up a critical position to surgery and yet be empowered through their informed and knowing choices to engage with it. If this is evidenced in empirical research it means that celebrations of a (decontextualised) reflexive, rational choice have been premature and have served to mask the 'conditions of choosing', specifically the processes of 'renewed objectification of female bodies' (Banet-Weiser and Portwood-Stacer 2006, 257) achieved in part by the current deployment of cosmetic technologies and the inciting, legitimising function of risk.

Conclusion

The processes of detraditionalisation and individualisation that characterise late modernity have firmly located biography construction onto the body, and specifically body projects, in ways unprecedented (Giddens, 1991; Shilling, 1993). While consumer culture encourages us to privilege appearance over other means of identity formation, bio-medical technological advances push the limits of what can be done and imagined for the body, leaving little refuge in a natural 'given' body (Negrin 2000). The enhanced body dominates our cultural symbolism and imaginary, rendering the modified body intelligible, acceptable and desirable. However the

---

7 The relationship between transformation, femininity and worth is exploited in the L'Oréal Paris advertising tag-line 'because you're worth it'.

extent to which the risks associated with cosmetic surgery are explained by the exercise of a knowing choice, serves to decontextualise the ways in which risks are understood, the function of cosmetic surgery as 'practices of the self' and relatedly, the very social meanings that socially embedded and, importantly, embodied women give both to self-work and their perception of risks therein.

In its aim to contextualise women's voluntary risk-taking, this chapter has argued that there are different pressures upon women's choices to face the inherent and well-publicised risks of cosmetic surgery. Not only do notions of ideal femininity define women's bodies as 'appropriate objects for this particular kind of medical intervention' (Davies 1995, 4), they also define the appropriateness and 'worth' of women in terms of appearance and increasingly, their levels of self-care and body-discipline (McRobbie 2004; Frost 2005). In addition there are the pressures of claiming and maintaining a biographical 'stake' through the exercise of choice in consumer capitalism. That cosmetic surgery can be marketed and experienced as an empowering means of securing a viable gendered self in the moral economy of neo-liberalism, suggests that the risks do not solely lie in the surgical event but in a rather more complex socio-cultural context whereby the 'risks' relate to losing or weakening viability in terms of dominant constructions of femininity and citizenship. These wider risks function to legitimise surgery as an approved mechanism to self-work in the cultural imaginary, and also allow academic attention to the suggestion that the risks to self lie in the decision *not* to enhance and rejuvenate the body.

References

Adams, M. (2003), 'The Reflexive Self and Culture: A Critique', *British Journal of Sociology* 54:2, 221–38.

Ashby, I. (2000), 'The Mutant Woman: The Use and Abuse of the Female Body in Performance Art', *Contemporary Theatre Review* 10:3, 39–51.

Ashikari, M. (2005), 'Cultivating Japanese Whiteness: The 'Whitening' Cosmetic Boom and Japanese Identity', *Journal of Material Culture* 10:1, 73–91.

Balsamo, A. (1996), *Technologies of the Gendered Body* (London: Duke University Press).

Banet-Weiser, S. and Portwood-Stacer, L. (2006), 'I Just Want To Be Me Again! Beauty Pageants, Reality Television and Post-Feminism', *Feminist Theory* 7:2, 255–72.

Beck, U. (1992), *Risk Society: Towards A New Modernity* (London: Sage).

Brandt, A. and Rozin, P. (eds) (1997), *Morality and Health* (London: Routledge).

Brannen, J. and Nilsen, A. (2005), 'Individualisation, Choice and Structure: A Discussion of Current Trends in Sociological Analysis', *The Sociological Review* 53:3, 412–28.

Cash, T. F. and Pruzinsky, T. (eds) (2002), *Body Image: A Handbook of Theory, Research and Clinical Practice* (New York: The Guilford Press).

Cruikshank, B. (1993), 'Revolutions Within: Self Government and Self Esteem', *Economy and Society* 22:3, 327–44.

Davies, K. (1995), *Reshaping the Female Body: The Dilemma of Cosmetic Surgery* (London: Routledge).

—— (2002). 'A Dubious Equality: Men, Women and Cosmetic Surgery', *Body and Society* 8:1, 49–65.

—— (2003), 'Surgical Passing or Why Michael Jackson's Nose Makes "Us" Uneasy', *Feminist Theory* 4:1, 73–92.

Dreyfuss, H. and Rabinow, P. (eds) (1982), *Beyond Structuralism and Hermeneutics* (Brighton: Harvester).

Epstein, D. and Steinberg, D. L. (1997) 'Love's Labours: Playing it straight on the Oprah Winfrey Show', in Steinberg, D.L. et al. (eds).

Epstein, D. and Steinberg, D. L. (1998), 'American Dreamin': Discoursing Liberally on the Oprah Winfrey Show', *Women's Studies International Forum* 21:1, 77–94.

Fitzpatrick, M. (2000), *The Tyranny of Health: Doctors and the Regulation of Lifestyle* (London: Routledge).

Foucault, M. (1982), 'The Subject and The Power', in Drefuss, H. and Rabinow, P. (eds).

—— (1986), *The History of Sexuality: The Care of the Self* (Harmondsworth: Penguin).

—— (1987), 'The Ethic of Care as a Practice of Freedom', *Philosophy and Social Criticism* 12:112–31.

—— (1988), 'Technologies of the Self', in Martin, L. et al. (eds).

Frost, L. (2005), 'Theorizing the Young Woman in the Body', *Body and Society* 11:1, 63–85.

Furedi, F. (2004), *Therapy Culture: Cultivating Vulnerability in an Uncertain Age* (London: Routledge).

Gagnè, P. and McGaughey, D. (2002), 'Designing Women: Cultural Hegemony and the Exercise of Power Among Women Who Have Undergone Elective Mammoplasty', *Gender and Society* 16:6, 814–38.

Gard, M. and Wright, J. (2005), *The Obesity Epidemic: Science, Morality and Ideology* (London: Routledge).

Galvin, R. (2002), 'Disturbing Notions of Chronic Illness and Individual Responsibility: Towards a Genealogy of Morals', *Health,* 6:2, 107–37.

Giddens, A (1991), *Modernity and Self Identity* (Cambridge: Polity Press).

Gill, R. et al. (2005), 'Body Projects and the Regulation of Normative Masculinity', *Body and Society* 11:1, 37–62.

Gordon, T. et al. (2005), 'Imagining Gendered Adulthood: Anxiety, Ambivalence, Avoidance and Anticipation', *European Journal of Women's Studies* 12:1, 83–104.

Green, E and Singleton, C. (2006), 'Risk Bodies at Leisure. Young Women Negotiating Space and Place', *Sociology* 40:5, 853–71.

Haiken, E. (1997), *Venus Envy: A History of Cosmetic Surgery* (Baltimore: Johns Hopkins University Press).

Hall, S. (2001), 'The Liposuction Scandal', *Guardian Unlimited* [website], (updated 8 June 2006) <http://www.guardian.co.uk/print/0,,4243899-103409,00.html>

Hall, S. (2006), 'Holidays For Plastic Surgery: Firm Under Fire', *Guardian Unlimited* [website], (updated 8 June 2006) <http://www.guardian.co.uk/print/0,,329481090-110418,00.html>

Hall, S. (2007), 'Doctors' Warning of Liposuction Op Rise by 90%', *Guardian Unlimited* [website], (updated 29 January 2007) <http://www.guardian.co.uk/print/0,,329699072-110418,00.html>

Hallowell, N. and Lawton, J. (2002), 'Negotiating Present and Future Selves: Managing the Risk of Hereditary Ovarian Cancer by Prophylactic Surgery', *Health* 6:4, 423–43.

Harrison, D. M. (2002), 'Rethinking Circumcision and Sexuality in the United States', *Sexualities* 5:3, 300–16.

Hazeldean, R. (2003), 'Love Yourself: The Relationship of the Self to Itself on Popular Self-Help Texts', *Journal of Sociology* 39:4, 413–28.

Jackson. S M. and Cram, F. (2003), 'Disrupting the Sexual Double Standard: Young Women's Talk About Heterosexuality', *British Journal of Social Psychology* 42:113–27.

Jeffreys, S. (2005), *Beauty and Misogyny: Harmful Cultural Practices in the West* (London: Routledge).

Katz, S. (2000), 'Busy Bodies: Activity, Ageing and the Management of Everyday Life', *Journal of Ageing Studies* 14:2, 135–52.

Lawler, S. (2005), 'Disgusted Subjects; The Making of Middle Class Identities', *The Sociological Review* 3:3, 429–46.

Lupton, D. and Tulloch, J. (2001) 'Border Crossings: Narratives of Movement, 'Home' and 'Risk', *Sociological Research Online* 5:4. <http://www.socresonline.org.uk/5/4/lupton.html>

—— (2002), 'Life Would Be Pretty Dull Without Risk: Voluntary Risk-Taking and Its Pleasures', *Health, Risk and Society* 4:2, 113–24.

McNay, L. (2000), *Gender and Agency* (Cambridge: Polity Press).

McRobbie, A. (2004), 'Notes on "What Not To Wear" and Post-Feminist Symbolic Violence', *The Sociological Review* 52:2, 97–109.

Martin, L. et al. (eds) (1988), *Technologies of the Self: A Seminar with Michel Foucault* (London: Tavistock).

Mills, A. (2002), 'The Dangers of Cosmetic Surgery and How to Minimise Them', *The Telegraph* [website] (updated 20 April 2007) <http://www.telegraph.co.uk/travel/main.jhtml?xml=travel/2002/03/09/etniptip.xml>

Millsted, R. and Frith, H. (2003), 'Being Large Breasted: Women Negotiating Embodiment', *Women's Studies International Forum* 26:5, 455–65.

Morgan. K. P. (1991), 'Women and the Knife: Cosmetic Surgery and the Colonization of Women's Bodies', *Hypatia* 6:3, 25–53.

Moss, J. (ed.) (1998), *The Later Foucault* (London:Sage).

Navarro, M. (2004),' The Most Private of Makeovers', *The New York Times* [website], (updated 1 December 2004) <http://nytimes.com/2004/11/28/fashion/28PLAS.html>

Negrin, L. (2000), 'Cosmetics and The Female Body: A Critical Appraisal of Poststructuralist Theories of Masquerade', *European Journal of Cultural Studies* 3:1, 83–101.

Nevin, L. (2006) The Third Leader; Skin Deep: *The Independent* 13 July.

Patton, W. and Mannison, M. (1998), 'Beyond Learning To Endure: Women's Acknowledge of Coercive Sexuality', *Women's Studies International Forum* 21:1, 31–40.

Petersen, A. (1997), 'Risk, Governance and the New Public Health', in Petersen, A. and Bunton, R. (eds).

Petersen, A. and Bunton, R (eds) (1997) *Foucault: Health and Medicine* (London: Routledge).

Pitts, V. (2003), *In the Flesh: The Cultural Politics of Body Modification* (Basingstoke: Palgrave).

Raisborough, J. (2006), 'Getting Onboard: Women, Access and Serious Leisure', *The Sociological Review* 54:2, 242–62.

Ramazanoglu, C. (ed.). (1993), *Up Against Foucault: Explorations of the Tensions Between Foucault and Feminism* (London: Routledge).

Sawicki, J. (1998), 'Feminism, Foucault and 'Subjects' of Power and Freedom', in Moss, J. (ed.).

Scraton, S. (1994). 'The Changing World of Women and Leisure: Feminism 'Postfeminism' and Leisure', *Leisure Studies* 13:4, 249–61.

Shilling, C. (1993), *The Body and Social Theory* (London:Sage).

Smart, B. (1998), 'Foucault, Levinas and the Subject of Responsibility', in Moss, J. (ed.).

Steinberg, D. L. et al. (eds) (1997), *Border Patrols: Policing the Boundaries of Heterosexuality* (London: Cassell Press).

Rose, N. (1999), *Governing The Soul: The Shaping of The Private Self* (London: Free Association).

Rosin, P. (1997), 'Moralization', in Brandt, A. and Rosin, P. (eds).

Sarwer, D. B. (2002), 'Cosmetic Surgery and Changes in Body Image', in Cash, F. and Pruzinsky, T. (eds).

Shilling, S. (1993), *The Body and Social Theory* (London: Sage).

Skeggs, B. (1997), *Formations of Class and Gender: Becoming Respectable* (London: Sage).

Tulloch, J. and Lupton, D. (2003), *Risk and Everyday Life* (London: Sage).

Weedon, C. (1997), *Feminist Practice and Poststructuralist Theory* (Oxford: Blackwell).

Chapter 3

'Fearing the Worst, Hoping for the Best': The Discursive Construction of Risk in Pregnancy

Dawn. S. Jones

Introduction

It has been argued that never before has pregnancy been considered such a risk-laden experience than it is today (Kitzinger 1991; Katz-Rothman 1994; Lesser et al. 2001; Ekberg 2007). In the shift to late modernity, with former certainties and securities challenged and undermined on a day-to-day basis, the experience of being pregnant and giving birth reflects precisely what Beck defines as 'reflexive modernization', with the need for individuals to 'produce, stage and cobble together their biographies themselves in the absence of fixed, obligatory and traditional norms and certainties' (Beck et al. 1994, 15). This chapter aims to explore the ways in which pregnant women receive and 'live out' discourses of risk in pregnancy in these times of uncertainty; it does so with specific focus on how women's everyday actions and experiences very much shape how such biographies are (re)constructed.

Continuing in the tradition of Lupton and Tulloch's (2002) 'case study' approach to risk in the everyday, I am interested in exploring how 'risk biographies' are *both* personalized, yet at the same time, as Beck et al. (2004) have argued, take place in the context of externally generated, scientifically-produced risk procedures. My research presented in this chapter details, through the use of focus groups, how women perceive and 'live through' the experience of undergoing screening and/ or diagnostic testing for foetal abnormalities.[1] I am interested in finding out what factors effect how women 'take stock' of the risks that they are presented with by medical professionals and how everyday knowledges and lived experience effect how such risks are received. In particular, the relation between medical definitions of risk (statistical) and that of the 'non-expert' is a key focus of the research.

---

1 Antenatal testing for my sample included maternal blood serum screening for chromosomal abnormalities (Down's, Edward's and Patou's syndromes), ultrasound screening (nuchal fold and 20-week anomaly scan), and diagnostic first/second trimester tests including amniocentesis and chorionic villus sampling.

This necessarily involves exploring the effect that existing knowledge, past experiences, and anecdotal accounts received from others might have in mediating the effect of the 'risk'. How the women in my sample have been effected during their pregnancies, and beyond, is also considered, suggesting that 'risk-labels' effect not only individuals as they are received, but have a lasting, longer-term effect on how lives are lived and futures are planned out. My findings suggest that while the women in my sample frequently utilised their own 'non-scientific' knowledges in 'making sense' of medical discourses; statistical risks are still considered the 'gold standard', having a validity and status that other discourses do not have. In this sense, while as Beck (1992) argues, science *is* increasingly questioned and challenged by the layperson, nonetheless, in the context of the insecurity that risk-testing generates, the reliance on expert opinions and reassurances is striking.

The chapter is structured as follows: below I outline the context in which my theorisation of risk develops and contributes to. My research method and methodology are then discussed, before presenting some of the contributions from participants in the focus groups. A low-level analysis of the themes emerging from the focus group is then provided, before a more-in-depth, theoretical commentary on how my research contributes to an understanding of risk and the everyday. I conclude by summarising my research findings and reflecting on the role of the individual in the formation of risk in late modernity.

Theorising Risk

My research into risk, pregnancy and the 'everyday' builds upon and in many ways contributes to Ulrich Beck's understanding of risk and what he has termed 'risk society' (1994; 2004). Risk is conceptualised by Beck as a socially constructed response to the uncertainties created and developed in and through modernization with everyday responses to ever-present 'risks' reflecting attempts by, for instance, governments and institutions, to govern and retain control over that which threatens our ontological security (Giddens 1990). As such, risk and how it is presented is very much dependent on decisions which are made in an attempt to calculate and rationalize away unpredictability and uncertainty (Beck 1992). In looking at the growth of the scientific community and, for the purposes of this research, the growth of antenatal screening programmes, it can be suggested, following Beck, that while there has been growing distrust of science and its predictions, so too, ironically, has our need for security and trust been needed more than ever. To quote from Beck on this, the insecurities of the new modernity mean that we '... end up with a world in which it is impossible not to make decisions, and it is impossible not to make them based on scientific reasoning' (2004, 203).

In examining how science relates, in these angst-ridden times, to the layperson, writers such as Beck (2004) and Giddens (1990) suggest that the traditional dichotomy between expert-knowledge and 'layperson' is under threat, with scientific knowledge revealed to be flawed and unstable. While the *desire* for objective knowledge and an accurate assessment of the 'real' risks that we face is greater than ever, the 'deconstruction' of the Scientific Establishment leaves a space in which, Beck et al. (2004) argue that individuals are left to reflexively piece together their places in the world, and as part of this, ascertain what the risks to their mental and physically well-being might actually be.

In examining the sphere of antenatal testing the desire to gain knowledge and certainty about the development of the foetus might be considered reflective of the desire to control and manage that which might be seen as a 'risk' to contemporary society – the birth of 'non-perfect', economically-draining human beings.[2] Furthermore, through implementing testing procedures to 'screen' and/or detect chromosomal abnormalities, risk testing might be considered a way of gaining ontological security in a sphere that has traditionally been left to 'fate'. However, in attempting to control the outcome of pregnancy through scientifically validated screening programmes, there is evidence that, as Beck (1992) suggests, such procedures actually *manufacture* risk, rather than responding to a risk that exists 'outside' of such tests. As the discussions from my focus group suggest, it is only *through* entering into the discourse of risk in agreeing to antenatal screening that, for many women, the 'risk' of carrying an abnormal foetus became apparent: in short, it is only through wanting to find out what one's risk might be, that the risk as such becomes 'knowable'. Consequently, when Beck et al. (1994) have written about the growth of the 'reflexive autobiography' as a reflection of the anxieties and insecurities that surround the manufacture of risk, so too can we link the degree of insecurity and anxiety experienced by women following antenatal screening, often for several months, sometimes years, to the desire by the scientific community and health care providers to manage the irrational and random nature of the natural world.

While antenatal testing might be presented by the medical profession as normalized and 'everyday', my research suggests, following Beck (1992), that the discourses and procedures that surround antenatal testing are at one level anything but routine and everyday; although the experiences of the women in my group are increasingly typical of those undergoing antenatal testing (Katz-Rothman 1994). Furthermore, my findings contribute to Beck's (2004) critique of science as 'god',

---

2 A government report into antenatal screening for Down's syndrome is suggestive of a governmental desire to 'hunt out' the Down's syndrome foetus as part of a cost-cutting exercise. To quote from the Government's report into Antenatal screening for Down's syndrome: 'In general, serum screening is more cost-effective than screening based on maternal; age alone at detection rates of about 50 per cent or greater. As the number of screening markers increases, the cost per pregnancy screened increases but, if an extra marker is sufficiently discriminatory, the cost per Down's syndrome birth avoided may decline. For example, the estimated cost per pregnancy screened and the cost per Down's syndrome birth avoided is: £8.90 and £25,600 for the double test; £9.60 and £22,700 for the triple test, and £11.60 and £23,100 for the quadruple test' (National Screening Committee 2003, 3).

suggesting that the traditional dichotomies between expert/layperson; science/myth; and objectivity/subjectivity are overly simplistic. Indeed, the need to gain certainty through testing, and the uncertainty that such testing creates, is seen here as one of the many contradictory consequences of the 'risk society' in late modernity.

Method and Methodology

My research involves the use of focus groups as a means of gaining information about women's risk perception. The use of focus groups was considered the preferred method for my research topic for a number of reasons: firstly, I believed that the attitudes and beliefs of the respondents would emerge through the social interaction that a group setting encourages, to a greater extent than, say, conducting face-to-face interviews (Silverman 2006). Secondly, I was able to gather a large amount of material in a relatively short period of time; with the views expressed in my data reflecting a 'multiplicity of views and emotional processes' (Gibbs 1997, 2). Thirdly, the use of the focus group enabled me to gain a deep insight into the shared nature of people's understandings of everyday life, and also how interaction in itself effects how views and opinions are expressed and communicated. Finally, it was felt that, while many of the women's experiences were of a highly personal nature, interacting in a group environment might encourage a 'community' feeling, perhaps allowing participants to 'open up' and confide in the group to a greater extent than might have occurred if a face-to-face interview, or indeed the survey method, had been used. As Kitzinger (1998) notes in her research that 'if a group works well, trust develops and the group may explore solutions to a particular problem as a unit' (cited in Gibbs 1997, 3).

Furthermore, Goss and Lienbach's (1996) suggestion (cited in McKinlay 2004) that there is potential for discursive communication to achieve a degree of empowerment for individuals, effecting not only the sentiments and feelings expressed within the group, but to have an effect on subsequent long-term social action beyond the limits of the group. Indeed, several members of the group admitted that their involvement in the research had been almost 'cathartic'; allowing them to admit to themselves the full effect of their experiences of antenatal testing.

The Focus Group: My Research Sample

The recruitment of participants for my focus group was achieved, in the main part, by word-of-mouth. I was familiar, through my own pregnancies, of existing social networks (for example, antenatal groups, friendships with women who have babies and/or young children), and was able to enlist several volunteers through the use of 'key informants' (Holbrook and Jackson 1996) that were known to me. Consequently, the final group consisted of individuals who were known, to varying degrees, to each other.[3] Such was the interest in my research topic that no incentive was required to recruit participants, although the practical organisation of the focus group was extremely difficult and time-consuming. When a day and venue were agreed, this would then have to be rescheduled several times due to the pressures of day-to-day life; for example, illness, family difficulties, work commitments, problems with travel arrangements. The final venue agreed upon was the house of my key-informant, with six participants out of the agreed eight able to meet on the specified date.

With all the participants having had some experience of antenatal testing in pregnancy, it was clear from the start that there were shared interests in those who had volunteered. All six participants were women with one, or more, children and were from middle-class professional backgrounds. All but one respondent worked outside of the home. Ages ranged from the late twenties to the mid forties years and all participants were of White-British ethnic origin. While it is acknowledged that my sample is hardly representative of the population, as it composed of middle-class, White women, there were advantages in having such a culturally-homogenous group. As Gibb argues,

> Participants need to feel comfortable with each other. Meeting with others whom they think of as possessing similar characteristics or levels of understanding about a given topic, will be more appealing than meeting with those who are perceived to be different (1997, 4).

Consequently, while the sample selected may have been too culturally homogenous to reveal a great diversity of opinions and beliefs, there were advantages too in selecting subjects who felt a degree of social ease with others in the group as this had the potential to facilitate a frank and honest discussion. It was hoped that a culturally cohesive group, with a degree of (perceived) like-mindedness on the selected topic would also potentially widen the range of responses given by individuals, releasing inhibitions, and possibly 'activating forgotten details of experience' (Catterall and Maclaren 1997, 1).[4]

Below, I draw out the key themes emerging from my data, with illustration from respondents' conversations where relevant.

---

3 In opposition to what Frey (1994) calls 'zero history groups', formed for a short-term project, my focus group, in consisting of individuals who know, or were known, to each other, provides interaction in a relatively 'natural' setting, as opposed to the 'laboratory' environment of some research groups.

4 Others have noted how participant interaction can encourage frank and open discussions. Hess (1968) for instance describes the benefits of group interaction as 'synergism, snowballing, stimulation, security, and spontaneity'. Others, such as Asbury (1995), argue that focus groups 'produce data rich in detail that are difficult to achieve with other research methods' (both cited in Catterall and Maclaren 1997, 1).

Initial Findings

Some initial points can be made regarding how risk discourses are received and 'made sense of' by the women in my focus group. The first point that can be made is that the risk statistics that women are presented with by the medical profession are generally accepted, with great weight given to the medial, scientific procedures that produced 'objective', hence accurate statistics. Indeed, while all but one of the participants received 'false positive' screening results, the scientific procedures through which the 'risk' is calculated were never questioned, with the outcome owing more to 'good fortune' than bad science.[5]

The interactive nature of the focus group discussion also illuminates what Douglas (1994, 14) has called the 'social solidarity' created when individuals who have felt threatened in some way, come together as a group. It was clear that, while extraordinary for each woman in the group, the fact that antenatal screening procedures resulted in similar degrees of anxiety and frustration for most in the group, provides evidence of the very 'everyday' nature of risk reception for pregnant women. While I develop later on an account of how women's reception of risk discourses contribute, or not, to a poststructuralist analysis of risk, it can be noted at this stage that women's individual reception of risk is very much shaped and controlled by the nature of the discursive site in and through which they come to negotiate what 'risk' means to them. For example, much was made of the use of the Internet and other media as a means of providing knowledge that would raise awareness of the procedures of antenatal testing. Interestingly, such 'discourses' provided knowledge for women that formed the basis of negotiation, even contestation, with the orthodox Medical Establishment that can be seen as potentially empowering when engaging with health professionals on a day-to-day basis.

Indeed, while 'risk' discourses certainly appear to have a 'special' status for the women in the sample, being associated with science, objectivity, and medical knowledge, nonetheless 'experiential' discourses gained from anecdotal stories, past experiences of the women themselves, and also the media, help to shape the context through which women build, and rebuild their own biographical stories of risk. In the section below, I consider the ways in which these 'biographies' are constructed and relayed to others, in more depth.

---

5 The accuracy of risk-calculation software has recently been investigated by the National External Quality Assessment System, in partnership with the National Screening Committee project team. The review demonstrated that 'even when consistent results are obtained for biochemical testing, significant differences occur in the risk estimate given to the woman when identical data are fed into the different software packages'. The report concluded that 'The feasibility of offering a personalised risk estimate will be explored' (National Screening Committee 2003, 14).

Low-level Analysis: Emerging Themes and Interpretation

In this section, I develop the very general points made above through identifying emerging themes that arose from the focus group discussion. Some 'low-level' analysis is provided, before attempting to place my findings in a wider theoretical context in the section which follows after.

Risk as Fact

There seems to be little, if any, discussion in the group of the socially constructed nature of the risk-calculation that women are presented with after undergoing maternal screening for foetal abnormalities. Throughout the discussion statistical figures are presented as existing in a vacuum, and not emerging from complex, frequently controversial scientific practices. This is illustrated in the following extracts taken from the group's conversation:

Jane: Once you hear the figures you don't really hear anything else ...

Emma: ... I'd definitely go for the nuchal next time ... much more accurate than those blood tests ...

Sarah: ... I'd definitely find out all the facts...

Jenny: There must be something wrong ... stats are hard and fast figures...

It is ironic that all but one of the participants received 'false positive'[6] outcomes of risk screening, yet the Medical Establishment and the science behind such tests is alluded to in the discussion as having an objective, almost god-like status, with the statistical figures interpreted in the context of the how the Medical Establishment 'reads' the risk. For instance, if the probability/statistical chance of having a baby with Down's syndrome is greater than 1 in 250 (for example 1 in 200 or 1 in 150) it is labelled 'screen positive' (ARC 2005). It would appear that the anxiety in my sample surrounding test results relates not simply to the statistical presentation itself, but to the labels 'screen positive', or 'screen negatives', which are applied to the results. Furthermore, as Kitzinger (1991) has argued, what it *is* that one is presented as being at risk *of* will also effect the reception of the risk discourse. Discourses of (ab)normality, disability, perfection, successful parenthood, for instance, all contribute to the construction of a culturally-symbolic space in which the birth

---

6 ARC (Antenatal Results and Choices) state on their website the facts about antenatal screening and false positives. To quote, 'Around 1 in every 20 women who have a blood serum screening test at 16 weeks for Down's syndrome will come back in the recall group. Of these 1 in 20 women, around 1 in 60 will have a baby with Down's syndrome. Of these 1 in 20 women, around 59 out of 60 will not have a baby with Down's syndrome' (ARC 2005).

of a child with 'abnormalities' is discursively synonymous with fear, disgust and embarrassment.

That said, the women in my sample did recognise that the science does involve subjective interpretations that can be incorrect. For example, when speaking of her experience of antenatal scans, Sarah said the following:

> We'd had a bit of dinner out with my boyfriend and his mum, chatting about finding out the sex and stuff, planning to stop off at Toys R Us on the way back to pick up some bits. I even remember arguing over how many piccies to ask for. I remember the doctor was running late, so his student whatever having a look first, then saying she needed to wait for him. She mumbled something about the liver, and he said he could see a white spot ... probably nothing he said but I remember really pushing him with what if ... so y'know turned out worst case scenario could mean brain damage [laughs] ... like GREAT! I had to have a blood test for an infection that would show up in the scan ... Bastards, three weeks of waiting to find out my results and they were fine! Turns out the spot was actually just outside the heart, which is normal and never even picked up on most scans ... [sighs]. I tell you what, there's something to be said to living years ago and finding out nothing! [from another participant] ... yeah, and then bleeding to death in a field.

Nevertheless, despite a challenge to the legitimacy of certain 'case by case' judgments that health professionals make, the established procedures through which the 'risks' are produced and disseminated are never challenged or critically examined by the women. The space in which risk is discussed and assessed appears almost as an effect or consequence of a set of objective testing procedures that stand 'outside', exterior to, the day-to-day experiences of experiencing and receiving risk 'results'.

Risk as Fear

Again, the discussion from the focus group very much implies that the fear and anxiety that antenatal testing might produce 'pre-exist' and are separate from the reception of such risk discourses. That the manufacture of the tests themselves and the procedures that take place in facilitating national screening programmes for the detection of abnormalities in pregnancy, do themselves arise out of a socially constructed space which reflect political and cultural norms, is never directly, or indirectly, alluded to. The following extracts from the focus-group discussion reflect this 'exteriorization' of the 'threat' posed by risk results:

Cathy : The letter came through just when I thought I was safe ...

Margaret: ... I still felt really anxious. The whole pregnancy had been spoilt ...

Anne: ... three weeks of waiting to find out my results and they were fine!

Emma: ... what price peace of mind?

Risk as Contestation

In contrast to the somewhat fixed nature of risk as it is seen here, the women in the group nonetheless partake in potentially empowering negotiation, even contestation, with both the meanings that are attached to risk when received (for example, accurate/ inaccurate tests), and the ways in which the medical establishment routinely deals with pregnancies which are classified as 'high risk' (including waiting times and hospital etiquette).

To quote:

Cathy: I remember going over and over the test results, scouring the web, printing out articles, searching and searching for stuff to make me feel better …

Margaret: I'd read about the FISH [fluorescent in situ hybridization] and took the page along with me to my amnio. They knew about it but didn't usually offer it … I was a bit annoyed with that 'cause if I hadn't read about it I'd have had to wait for 2 weeks [for results …

Jenny: I was straight onto the net for general knowledge rather than reassurances. Other people's stories really helped too. Everyone seemed to know someone who had been through it and had come out the other side alright … I suppose I felt I'd taken a bit more control, but I still felt really anxious …

Jane: Yeah, I'd definitely go for the nuchal next time … much more accurate than those blood tests.

Nicola: … I'd definitely find out all the facts, go onto the internet and that so I know what I'm talking about. Not just walk into it blindfolded.

It would appear that the procedures and categorisations associated with receiving a 'high risk' screening result are talked through and investigated by women as a means of feeling in control and fully-informed about the 'risks' that they are facing. Such strategies do not extend to a critique of the procedures by and through which risks are manufactured by the medial establishment. Risk negotiation/contestation as an everyday practice may empower the individual through the knowledges that they acquire, yet my data indicates that this 'empowerment' works only as a means of coping and 'living through' the experiences that being labelled as at 'high risk' bring. The processes by which such calculations are arrived at remain, for the women, very much removed from the everyday, exhibiting a space that is considered separate from, external to, the world in which risks are received.

Risk Avoidance

The effects of 'high-risk' labelling on pregnancies would appear to be long-term, shaping the ways in which pregnancies are remembered, and affecting the ways in which subsequent pregnancies, real or planned, are lived out. There is strong evidence, from the conversations that took place in the focus group, that what have become everyday decisions for pregnant women regarding procedures for antenatal screening are, as a result of former 'risk-labelling', problematised on many levels. In signifying risk testing in such a way; past experiences for some create a desire to *avoid* any future risks, as seen in the following extracts:

> Margaret: We wouldn't have anything [tests]… it's not worth the stress, and to be honest, we'd have whatever we were given anyway …

> Jane: … I tell you what, there's something to be said to living years ago and finding out nothing!

> Cathy: [on subsequent pregnancy] NO way was I having ANY tests that time though!

> Sarah: No tests, not after all that. What's meant to be will be. I mean it's still your baby. I really think they go into things in too much detail; they take the magic away for us.

One of the striking juxtapositions of how women perceive risk in pregnancy can be noted here. Whereas for some, any problems that exist with testing procedures are pragmatic in nature (not enough information; need for the 'best' tests available); for others freedom from future anxiety and uncertainties that testing throws up is found through retreating into the sphere of fate, where decisions and outcomes become associated more with the 'pre-modern' ('fate', 'nature') than science and medicine.

For those choosing the latter option, it is the *experience* of antenatal testing for foetal abnormality that is to be feared and not any 'abnormality' that may be identified. Ironically, it is the process of screening *for* risk that is considered 'risky' for some women in the group, with risk avoidance seeming a logical reaction to experiences of 'illogical' (false positive) screening results. Thus while is might be considered by those in the medical profession 'risky' *not* to find out the statistical possibility that one might be carrying an abnormal foetus, especially if a member of a 'high risk' group; for some women the chance that screening might 'spoil the pregnancy' through the anxieties it creates, is too great a price for pay for finding out the 'truth'.

So how do the merging themes listed above 'fit' with theoretical frameworks for understanding risk perception in everyday life? In the late-modern era, risk is an ever-present characteristic in everyday living, and it would seem that the experience of pregnancy is no exception. With a shift away from the certainties and assurances that Science and medicine might once have had, existing as meta-narratives that shape, in a top-down way, the ways in which 'healthcare' is experienced, the narrative of everyday life is now seemingly contested. As Beck has argued, the certainty that was once attached to the 'scientific' is now under question, with reflexive modernisation creating a situation where scientists, health care practitioners, and politicians are increasingly subject to challenge and contestation (2004, 203).

That the scientific community is increasingly vulnerable can be extended to the practices of antenatal testing for abnormalities in pregnancy. As Beck has argued, risk should be seen as a systematic way of coping with uncertainty and insecurity created by modernisation itself (2004). As such, the development of more accurate ways in which to identify 'affected' pregnancies by scientists may be seen as a means by which science can be said to cope, in a rational way, with the uncertainties of nature. For instance, in offering a test that will produce a quantitative 'risk' calculation from a simple blood test, might in itself be considered one way of making sense of the unpredictable; allowing the 'everyday' to continue in a secure and controlled environment. Ironically, my findings suggest that the ways in which women 'receive' such test results, and 'live out' for themselves the narratives that such risk discourses 'throw up' is more suggestive of the creation of an 'everyday' narrative that becomes increasingly characterized by insecurity, and anxiety.

It is clear that the 'individual', as Beck (1992) suggests, is increasingly characterised as responsible for 'taking stock' of the risks that they are presented within pregnancy. The social experience of pregnancy becomes, in a sense, controlled by the environment in which risk discourses are manufactured, and yet, as Tulloch and Lupton (2003) make clear in their work, the individual is herself left to negotiate the signification of such discourses. My findings suggest that a number of factors effect how individual 'biographies' are created: such as the amount of pre-existing knowledge a woman has about the testing procedures; and past experiences and anecdotal stories. Yet, as Beck (1992) has argued, there continues a degree of 'fixity' as to the role that science and the medial establishment plays. As Giddens (1990) has suggested, while individuals do indeed 'act out' the role that poststructuralists 'assign' to them, actively interpreting and contesting the information with which they are presented; nonetheless science and the risks it calculates continues, for the women in my sample, to have a 'special' status. The risks are seen as potentially contestable, especially when selecting the 'type' of test to have, to be 'tested' (or not), and how to deal with the consequences of a 'high' risk finding. However, the actual processes by which risks are 'produced' in the laboratory and/or computer lab remain unchallenged. The status of the scientific institution as provider of both initial 'screening' results, and diagnosis of 'actual' risk, maintains to some extent the reputation of 'science as god', with risks seen as 'real', objective, and reflective of the 'true' status of one's pregnancy. That all but one of the women in my sample received 'false positives' from their screening blood test does not in any way compromise for such individuals the validity and accuracy of the ways in which risk is 'produced'. In short, the fact that antenatal risk results are themselves the outcome of a socially-constructed set of computer-based programmes recognised by scientists as themselves vulnerable to errors,[7] is not knowledge that relates in any way to how

---

7 'Inaccurate' results are also produced by the failure of antenatal tests to 'personalise' the context in which testing takes place. For example, body weight of the pregnant women; date of last menstrual period; the occurrence of first trimester bleeding; number of foetuses

women themselves perceive risk in pregnancy; the discovery that one's risk statistic is in fact a 'false positive' becomes a matter of relief and good fortune, and not a cause of irritation and scepticism of the testing procedure *per se*.

We have then a situation where modernist beliefs (such as faith in science) coexist alongside a late-modernist environment in which the *meanings* of such 'risk labels' are indeed negotiated by individuals as part of the everyday experience of being pregnant.

Conclusion

What, then, can we conclude about the ways in which risks are received and 'lived out' by women in pregnancy? How are risk discourses drawn upon, and what status can we give such discourses in shaping the space in which women come to construct their biographies? My research is suggestive of the following points. First, there is a sense in which women occupy relatively 'fixed' identity positions in agreeing to undergo maternal serum screening in pregnancy. Regardless of any desire to unpack and deconstruct the space in and through risks operate, the role of the 'patient' continues to be, to some extent, 'pre-set' by the medical institution; with little chance to challenge directly the subject position that one is placed in. Second, that while testing is presented to women as a rational, sensible, and reinsuring process, that the *reception* of risk results – especially those that are coded as 'high risk' – becomes anything but rational when received in a social-cultural context of 'abnormality' and 'disability'. In short, the possible consequences of being 'the one' that is indeed carrying the 'abnormal' foetus, is very much magnified by the cultural consequences in late-modern society of giving birth to, and bringing up, a child with learning disabilities/special needs and magnifies further the anxiety felt by those who are living the 'risk', even when such risks are statistically negligible.

It is clear from my research that the women from my focus group are at the centre of the risk scenario that each has found themselves in. While the power relations that surround and contain the ways in which tests come to be available (or not) to women, retains a certain fixity, the space in which risks are received, talked and lived through, on a day-to-day basis, is very much characterised by a good degree of fluidity. Risk, while perceived by women as having an 'objective' status, nonetheless becomes meaningful to each individual woman in a variety of ways, suggesting that risk, at the level of the everyday at least, must be considered a highly subjective social process. As Lupton and Tulloch (2001) have argued, risk is indeed very much to be seen as an *effect* of various discourses, with actions that stem from risk results

---

present; and the time at which the test is conducted, will all impinge of the 'accuracy' of the risk statistic that is produced. The National Screening Committee (2003) is currently considering the feasibility of providing personalized risk estimates for pregnant women undergoing antenatal screening for chromosomal abnormalities in pregnancy.

(for instance, further testing) in a sense 'set in motion' by the discursive context in which such risk discourses are produced in the first place. In short, the 'self' is very much an outcome of the ways in which individuals relate to, and make sense of, the discursive 'risk label' that they have been given, often defining not only the memory of the whole pregnancy, but the identity that women give to themselves during the pregnancy, and indeed in subsequent pregnancies too. Clearly, as Adam (2003) has suggested, the model of the rational social actor, engaging in a consensual way with the procedures and demands of the medial establishment, does not exist in the context of my research findings. Instead, whether it is through a quest to 'legitimise' (or not) their 'risk label' through searching for alternative knowledge sources, or attempting to 'guide' the medical establishment through challenging the 'accepted' route of risk testing, women do seek to 'personalise' their degree of 'risk', albeit in a context in which Science continues to play a key role.

As Beck (1992) has argued, it appears that the individual is located in a contradictory social space in late modernity, reflected in and through the ways in which 'risk' is played out in our everyday lives. With knowledge forms, identities, and social roles consistently challenged, there is a sense in which we seek security from wherever that security is offered, whether that is from medical science or in alternative knowledge forms provided by, for instance, anecdotal narratives and internet websites. Indeed, in seeking to have secure, 'safe' and risk-free pregnancies, women are drawn towards testing procedures that seek to 'reassure' by providing 'objective' testing for abnormalities. And yet in submitting to such testing, as a means of reaching a sense of security, many women find risk testing does itself become a risk-laden process. While my research does, then, suggest a very personal relationship to risk in the context of reflexive modernisation, with individual biographies of risk very much now part of the 'everyday' process of being pregnant, institutional practices and expert knowledges continue to shape and even legitimise the ways in which individuals reflexively live out risk and the anxieties that it generates.

References

Adam, B. (2003), 'Reflexive Modernization Temporalized', *Theory, Culture and Society* 20:2, 59–78.

Antenatal Results & Choices [website], (updated 31 May 2005) <http:///www.arc-uk.org/index.html>

Beck, U. (1992), *Risk Society: Towards a New Modernity* (London: Sage).

—— et al. (1994), *Reflexive Modernisation: Politics, Tradition and Aesthetics in the Modern Social Order* (Cambridge: Polity).

—— with Williams, J. (2004), *Conversations with Ulrich Beck* (Cambridge: Polity).

Catterall, M. and Maclaren, P. (1997), 'Focus Group Data and Qualitative Analysis Programs: Coding the Moving Picture as Well as the Snapshots', *Sociological Research Online*, 2:1, <http://www.socresonline.org.uk/socresonline/2/1/6.html>

Douglas, M. (1994), *Risk and Blame: Essays in Cultural Theory* (London: Routledge).

Ekberg, M. (2007), 'Maximizing the Benefits and Minimizing the Risks Associated With Prenatal Genetic Testing', *Health, Risk and Society* 9:1, 67–81.

Frey, L. R. (1994), 'The Naturalistic Paradigm: Studying Small Groups in the Postmodern Era', *Small Group Research* 25:4, 551–77.

Gibbs, A. (1997) 'Focus Groups', *Social Research Update* University of Surrey [website], (updated 15 September 2005) <http://sru.soc.ac.uk/SRU19.html>

Giddens, A. (1990), *The Consequences of Modernity* (Cambridge: Polity).

Katz-Rothman, B. (1994), *The Tentative Pregnancy: Amniocentesis and the Sexual Politics of Motherhood* (London: Rivers Oram Press).

Kitzinger, J. (ed.) (1998), *Developing Focus Group Research: Politics, Theory and Practice* (London: Sage).

Kitzinger, S. (1991), *Rediscovering Birth* (London: Little Brown).

Holbrook, B. and Jackson, P. (1996), 'Shopping Around: Focus Group Research in North London', *Area* 28:2, 136–42.

Lesser, Y. et al. (2001), 'Elective Amniocentesis in Low-Risk Pregnancies: Decision Making in the Era of Information and Uncertainty', *American Journal of Public Health* 91:4, 639–41.

Lupton, D. and Tulloch, J. (2001), 'Border Crossings: Narratives of Movement, 'Home' and 'Risk', *Sociological Research Online* 5:4. <http://www.socresonline.org.uk/5/4/lupton.html>

—— (2002), 'Life Would Be Pretty Dull Without Risk: Voluntary Risk-Taking and Its Pleasures', *Health, Risk and Society* 4:2, 113–124.

National Screening Committee (2003) *Antenatal Screening for Down's Syndrome – Policy & Quality Issues* (London: Department of Health).

McKinlay, I. (2004), 'Social Work and Sustainable Development: An Exploratory Study'. University of Pretoria [website], (updated 27 November 2006) <http://upetd.up.ac.za/thesis/available/etd-09272004-113416/unrestricted/08appendices.pdf>

Silverman, D. (2006), *Interpreting Qualitative Data*, 3rd Edition (London: Sage).

Tulloch, J. and Lupton, D. (2003), *Risk and Everyday Life* (London: Sage).

Chapter 4

P.E. Kits, Playgrounds and Pain: An Exploration of Children's Experiences of Risk, Pain and Injury in Sport

Lara Killick

Introduction

> It's [risk] all part of life, I mean ... even when you're walking around, you're gonna fall over and hurt yourself? So what's the point? What you gonna do, like wrap yourself in bubble wrap or something, It's just pointless. Especially if you are going to play a game, if you really want to go for it, then go for it and if you get hurt then that's just one thing that's going to happen. Don't waste your time thinking about it (Ife, eleven year old school girl).

Sport has long been identified by governments and other organisational bodies as an appropriate agent in addressing various 'social problems' from rising crime rates to international political unrest. Yet it becomes apparent that public policies which utilise sport as a means to tackle these social 'ills' are premised on a very one-sided perception of sport. That is, they emphasise the perceived health and social benefits of sporting cultures while largely ignoring the associated risks of continued sporting participation. While such a functionalist viewpoint of sport is not wholly inaccurate it does downplay and marginalise the existence of more damaging aspects of sport (for example long-term injury, recourse to drugs) and the debilitating effect these may have on the participant's physical, mental and social health.

It is necessary to understand these potentially damaging dimensions of sports participation given sport's central position in educational curricula across the Western World and the volume of children who participate in sporting activities on a regular basis. Furthermore, sport is accorded a major role in the promotion of health and the attainment of a 'healthy lifestyle' in the UK based upon perceived positive health benefits[1] (Department of Health 2005). But what if assumptions about the possible health benefits of sports participation do not adequately reflect the complex and often conflicting relationships between sport, health and risk? The unproblematic

---

1 Sport England's (2005) website asserts that regular participation in sport can improve physical fitness and psychological well-being; boost social capacity and cohesion; reduce crime and improve community safety; and facilitate life-long learning.

acceptance of a positive causal link between sport and health may have significant implications for children's short-term and long-term health. This chapter offers the opportunity to explore differences in the *rhetoric* surrounding the positive causal link between sport and health and the *actual* lived experiences of those children involved in regular sporting activity, many of whom are involved in activities which may place their physical, psychological, social and moral health at risk.

Current sociological research suggests that adult sports participation may be occurring in a cultural context that 'glorifies risk, normalises injury, accepts pain and encourages individuals to play whilst injured' (Nixon 1994, 79). Many sociologists of sport have used Howard Nixon's pioneering work in the field, completed in America in the early 1990s, as a point of departure and a substantial body of work dedicated to the risk-pain-injury nexus now exists (see Connell 1990; Curry 1993; Curry and Strauss 1994; Young et al. 1994; Young and White 1995; Walk 1997; Roderick et al. 2000; Malcolm and Sheard 2002; Pike and Maguire 2003; Safai 2003; Howe 2004; Young 2004; Loland et al. 2006).

Despite the rapid growth in research dedicated to sports-related risk, pain and injury it has become clear that 'the physically and emotionally painful ramifications of injury for young and child athletes, and the extent to which sport might be abusive to children's bodies, has been almost entirely ignored' (Young 2004,18). This chapter begins efforts to address this disparity in research. It draws on data collected from eight hundred and fifty-two school children during a three month research study. Beginning with an overview of the methodological framework utilised, this chapter will then present a brief summary of the sports-specific literature surrounding risk experiences. Specific attention will be paid to the work of Nixon (1993; 1994; 1996) whose primary contribution rests in his identification of a widespread 'culture of risk' in modern elite sports cultures. Underpinned by empirical evidence, efforts will then be made to critically engage with the existing literature to make sense of the cultural context of children's compulsory sports participation and more specifically, children's lived everyday experience of sports-related 'risks'.

Methodological Framework

The theoretical foundations of my work are located in figurational (process) sociology; accordingly a multi-method approach to data collection was utilised. Derived from the work of Norbert Elias, figurational theory encourages researchers to re-orientate many of their sociological assumptions; moving from static dichotomies (such as traditional understandings of agency-structure) towards a more processual model, which emphasises notions of interdependence, dynamic relations and long-term social processes (see Mennell and Goudsblom 1998; Van Krieken 1998; Elias 2000). The re-orientation of traditional dichotomies carries a number of methodological implications. For the purposes of this chapter the most significant of these implications are the dissolution of divergent categories of qualitative and quantitative methodology and the advocation of a multi-strategy approach. In light of this, both self-report questionnaires and semi-structured interviews were undertaken to generate data on children's perception and 'everyday' experiences of sports-related risks.

Data was collected from six secondary schools located in the 'Churchill' area of England.[2] The schools involved in the study covered the broad spectrum of school types evident in England (including co-educational, single-sex, state and fee-paying institutions) and all the participants were in Year Eight (11–12 year olds). A fifteen-item self report questionnaire was distributed during the school's morning registration period and a response rate of 98 per cent was achieved (n=852). Data was collected from both female (n=466) and male (n=386) pupils. The questionnaire was intended to develop an insight into children's lived experiences of their sports participation. Initial questions were dedicated to gaining an understanding of the types of sports they participated in; the standard and frequency at which they took part; and their exposure to, and engagement with, sport through means other than their own participation, for example, through the mass media. The children were then asked to provide information about whether they had experienced any pain or injuries as a result of their sports participation; the kind of injuries they encountered; and their response to these injuries. The closing questions related to their emotional response to injuries; their perception of sports-related risks; and the influence of 'significant others'.

Upon receipt, the questionnaires were categorised according the child's level of participation in sport. At each school, two children from each category of participation (rated from 'school P.E. only' through to 'national level' sporting participation) were then selected for interview. Semi-structured interviews were conducted with forty of the participants. The primary aim of the interviews was to 'yield rich insights into [the children's] biographies, experiences, opinions, values, aspirations and attitudes' (May 2001, 120). A number of topics from the questionnaire provided a thematic guide for the interview and the researcher was able to expand on the answers provided whilst simultaneously gaining clarification and meaning to the responses given. Of significant importance was the ability of the children to discuss topics using their own frames of reference, for example, using their own definitions of 'risk' or 'injury', thus preventing the preconceptions of the (adult) researcher from gaining dominance. The sociological purpose of exploring children's perception of risk, pain and injury across a broad range of sports and levels of participation was to:

---

2 In addition to the development of ethical research tools which must be undertaken in all forms of social research, specific ethical requirements in line with child protection legislation must also be addressed when children are the focus of any project (Greig and Taylor 1999). As such, ethical considerations at every stage of the research process were led by the Statement of Ethical Practice for the British Sociological Association. Deputy Head Teachers and Head teachers of P.E. acted as gatekeepers to the sample and approved the content of the questionnaires. Furthermore, questionnaires were distributed via official school channels and informed parental consent was obtained for each interview.

account more fully for the diversity, contradiction, and ambiguity which research to date indicates is likely to be a central characteristic of ... sports related pain and injury experiences (Charlesworth and Young 2004, 164).

A Sporting 'Culture of Risk'

Academic literature has begun to build a robust case for the existence of what has been termed a 'culture of risk' in relation to certain adult sport subcultures, particularly those at an elite level (see Nixon 1993; Walk 1997; Howe 2004; Young 2004). Nixon is responsible for much of the early research on a sporting risk-pain-injury nexus and his work has provided the catalyst for a substantial amount of further study into the normalisation of injury, glorification of pain and rationalisation of risk within sport (see Young 2004; Loland et al. 2006).

It is important here to draw attention to a conceptual difficulty that arise from Nixon's use of the term 'risk. Nixon utilises a definition that appears relatively narrow in its understanding of sports-related risk. That is, it prioritises physical risk at the expense of a multi-dimensional understanding of sports-related risks. When exploring sports-related risks there is a tendency to overemphasise the physical risks in sport as they are visible, tangible and have clear consequences for the health of the athlete/child in question. However, involvement in sport, or more specifically curtailed involvement in sport may have powerful and significant social implications for the individual. The risk of damage to their social identity may be a potent and commanding factor in the individual's risk-pain-injury experiences. So while, bodily risk has garnered a great deal of attention in the literature on sports-related risks, it seems incumbent that we also tease out the plurality of 'other' risks that are embedded in sports contexts and move towards an understanding of risk that reflect the complexity of these experiences.

That said a primary contribution made by Nixon is his identification of a 'culture of risk' which, he argues, is apparent in many modern sporting subcultures. He defines the 'culture of risk' as:

A set of mediated beliefs about structural role constraints, structural inducements, general cultural values, and processes of institutional rationalisation and athletic socialisation that collectively convey the message that they ought to accept the risks, pain and injuries of sport (Nixon 1993, 188).

There appears to be three core elements of a sporting 'culture of risk'; the rationalisation of risk, the normalisation of injury and the glorification of pain. The collective effect of which is the athletes' conclusions that playing through pain and with injury is their own viable option if they wish to continue to participate.

Nixon draws attention to a 'conspiratorial alliance' of coaches, athletic administrators and sports medicine personnel whose actions perpetuate the 'peculiar and persuasive' acceptance of pain and risk in sport (Morris 1991, 182). Moreover, he demonstrates how patterns of interactions and power relations within a sports network ('sportsnet') mediate the core elements of a 'culture of risk'. It is through these 'conspiratorial alliances', Nixon (1994) argues, that athletes are exposed to mediated, and more direct, messages that encourage them to play through pain and with injuries for as long as possible. We can observe the character of athletes who endure pain, make sacrifices for the team and ignore the personal consequences of playing with injuries frequently being glorified and heroicised by coaches, team-mates, supporters and the media. However those athletes who chose to talk openly about their pain and injuries or those who remain on the sidelines for long periods of time risk stigmatisation, especially if the pain and injuries have invisible sources (Nixon 1994).

In addition, Nixon (1994) asserts that interactions within these networks reinforce a specific ideology surrounding the image of a 'successful athlete'. Athletes are immersed in the rhetoric of producing winning teams and maintaining an identity consistent with being a successful athlete with little consideration for the personal risks they are taking with their bodies and future health. It is here that we can link Nixon's (1994) observations with Hughes and Coakley's concept of a prevalent 'sports ethic'. Coakley (2003, 168) identifies the 'sport ethic' as an unwritten:

> Set of norms that many people, in power and performance sports, have accepted as the dominant criteria for defining, what it means to be an athlete and to successfully claim an identity as an athlete.

It involves an unquestioned commitment to and over-acceptance of, the norms and rules of sporting subcultures and is considered a form of positive deviance in sport (Hughes and Coakley 1991). Research completed by Ewald and Jiobu (1985, 310) concluded that elite athletes often 'zealously pursued and over-conformed to the norms within their sports groups to such an extent that their sports participation was disruptive to their physical health and personal comfort'; indicating that positive deviance is not an uncommon phenomenon in sport.

Hughes and Coakley (1991, 309) identify four critical elements they believe constitute and define the 'sports ethic':

1. An athlete makes sacrifices for 'the game'.
2. An athlete strives for distinction.
3. An athlete accepts risks and plays through pain.
4. An athlete accepts no limits in the pursuit of possibilities.

The key observation to draw from this set of beliefs is that the acceptance of risk, pain and the normalisation of injury are considered integral parts of a sports performer's identity, of being perceived as a sports performer by others and obtaining success as a sporting individual. Hughes and Coakley (1991) argue that the 'sports ethic' drives athletes to continue through pain, to dismiss injury as a limiting factor in performance and to make sacrifices with their body in the pursuit of excellence. For example, Andrew Flintoff describes a period in his sporting career, where:

> Despite the major discomfort I was feeling, I was playing alright going into the Test series against India at Lord's. But the pain just got worse and went from being merely uncomfortable to absolute agony. By the time I got to Trent Bridge I could barely walk and needed Rachel [his wife] to fasten my laces. But I had more injections in my backside and bowled a lot of overs, despite being in bits (Flintoff 2005, 118).

Dominique Moceanu, a fourteen-year-old gymnast in the 1996 US Olympic team competed with a four-inch stress fracture in her right leg because, she explained 'What else can I do? I have to bite my teeth somehow and make it through. This is the Olympics you're talking about here' (Coakley 1998:153). Coakley (2003) stresses that those who do not appear to make these physical sacrifices fail to be labelled 'real' athletes.

A willingness to confront, overcome and accept fear and the risk of injury is therefore central to being labelled a 'committed athlete'. Research suggests that elite athletes do not consider subscription to the 'sports ethic' a form of deviance, but rather that it is a means of confirming and reconfirming their identities as athletes and their membership in the group (Colburn 1985). Whilst adherence to a 'culture of risk' and 'sports ethic' encourages athletes to accept risk-taking in sport and downplays the consequences of injury, neither protect the athletes from the physically, socially, economically, or emotionally debilitating consequences of chronic pain and serious injury.

From Playground to Test Arena: The Permeation of a 'Culture of Risk'

Various sociologists have suggested that the 'culture of risk' is deeply embedded in sporting subcultures and is particularly prevalent in sporting environments where athletes have been seriously involved in sport at elite levels and for longer time periods (Hughes and Coakley 1991; Coakley, 2003; Howe 2004; Young 2004; Loland et al. 2006). Moreover, they argue that elite sports performers are more likely to be immersed in the 'culture of risk' since their identities, statuses and livelihoods are dependent on their performance and the ability to remain functional on the sports field. However, these athletes form a small minority of the millions who regularly participate in sport across the globe. Questions need to be raised in relation to the over six million children in England who take part in various forms of sport every week as part of their compulsory educational curricula (National Audit Office 2005). Is it appropriate to utilise Nixon's concept of a 'culture of risk' and the associated 'sports ethic' to make sense of the cultural context of compulsory school sport? The following sections of this chapter will address some of the key findings which emerged from the research data.

'You take that risk when you play a physical sport, things like that just happen': Children's Perception of Sports-related Risk

Where existing research draws attention to the various techniques of rationalisation used by adult athletes (see Young 2004) the data surrounding children's perception of sports-related risks raises some interesting discussion points. The first is concerned with notions of individualisation and control. When asked to provide examples of what they considered 'risky' activities, the children made reference to discourses of risk associated with contemporary moral panics around health, where risky behaviours are seen to have clear outcomes (Rich and Evans 2005; Evans et al. 2003). These include 'going out with friends but not telling anyone where we are going' (Lauren); 'smoking and drugs' (Sarah); and 'getting fat and lazy, you know, 'cause then you might get a heart attack' (Tom). In this context, 'risk' is understood within a discourse of individualism, whereby the individual is able to control the outcomes of particular 'risky' encounters through their actions.

Conversely, we observe children attaching the physical risks involved in sport as something outside of human control; they become conceptualised as 'bad luck' or 'something that just happens'. For example, Matt, a club level rugby player, described risk as 'something that is dangerous, something that means I will get hurt' but continued to explain that:

> rugby isn't risky, we have referees and rules and they stop the game being risky. Sometimes, I guess it can be dangerous, but only if someone is not playing fair, like what happened to Brian O'Driscoll [2005 Lions rugby captain] two weeks ago, or if the referee is rubbish and letting the players get away with loads.

Risk, in the sporting context, becomes something that happens 'to them' rather than something they 'allow' to happen to them. Ownership and responsibility of risk is perceived to lie outside of the individual, for example with the referees or other players. Yet when the consequences of the risks become 'real', for example when a player is 'spear tackled' and left with severe damage to their neck and shoulder region, management of it immediately becomes the responsibility of the individual. The consequence of risk, the physical injury and embodied pain is literally 'owned by' the individual, a stark contrast to the perceived relationship between risk-individual prior to the tackle.

Shame, Guilt and Frustration: The Emotional Response to Injury

Empirical data suggests that the 'culture of risk' fosters very specific emotional responses in athletes when they are out of action following an injury. Guilt, shame, uncertainty and frustration are frequently reported in the athletes' discussions of their periods of inactivity (Nixon 1994; Pike and Maguire 2003). Such emotions are not limited to those athletes at the peak of their career who stand to experience financial loss from their inactivity, but also those athletes who consider their sports participation a form of recreation (Pike and Maguire 2003). The children presented similar emotional responses, most notably frustration and anger. Tom, who spent three and a half weeks out of action with a sore neck, spoke of being 'annoyed, frustrated that I couldn't play sport'. Equally Sarah explained 'it was annoying, because I was just sitting at home thinking I could be playing'.

The data suggested that the degree of frustration felt is heightened as you move along the participation continuum. For example, during the interviews two children from the 'compulsory sport only' end of the continuum talked of injury as 'painful, but I like the rest, and I get a lot of sympathy' (Amy). Furthermore Tim explained that 'well, if I am injured and we have got rugby then it means I don't have to "forget my P.E. kit", I do that a lot'. This contrasted strongly with Caitlin, a national gymnast, who told of how she:

> hate[s] being injured and not being able to do anything. I miss training; I miss the feeling of competing, of being part of the team and of being ok. It's just so frustrating, sitting on the side and not being able to do it.

In addition, many of the children spoke of periods of inactivity as a time of isolation and uncertainty.

> Eddie: I didn't really feel part of the team, I felt a bit isolated. I was sort of over in the corner, watching as people were sort of passing it [the ball] around, laughing, joking and I could have been part of that.

> Jessica: It felt weird not playing, not being with my friends. I wasn't really sure what to do with my time, TV got boring and I hated having to sit and watch everyone else have fun.

Interestingly, however such emotional experiences did not result in the children exhibiting signs of fear or worry over the possibility of injury. When asked to describe their pre-participation thoughts, talk related to fear of injury was notably absent. The children spoke of controlling their nerves, 'I am always very nervous, I need to pretend that no one is watching, so I think about being calm' (Chloe); the tactical requirements of their performance, '[I think about] trying to put in a big tackle; communication, getting the team spirits up, just trying to focus really' (James); and personal achievement, 'I think about how it feels to score a goal, and how I will celebrate it this game, everyone likes my celebrations, they make them laugh' (Josh). If discussions turned to the topic of injury the children responded with comments such as:

> Joe: Yeah, but you can't spend all your life wondering if you might get hurt, otherwise you wouldn't do anything ... there is no point in worrying about it because if you want to do it [sport] then you just have to, you just have to face the consequences.

'Playing hurt'

'Playing hurt' also constitutes a central aspect of Nixon's (1994) model and frequent references were made in the interviews to playing through pain and with injuries. James described one incident:

> Well, my dodgy knees, they always hurt but I never got them checked out, then one match they just went. Every time I ran it felt like my knee was just about to snap, but I needed to play, I was captain and there was no way I was going to come off.

Again, the frequency with which children reported playing through painful experiences, and with sports-related injuries, appeared to increase as the child moved along the participation continuum. It is here that it is appropriate to emphasis links with Hughes and Coakley's (1991) 'sports ethic' and the proposed existence of a dominant athletic identity.

The children placed a high regard on 'dedication' and 'commitment', central to which they placed the notion of 'playing hurt'.

> Tim: I like players who are dedicated, committed, you know, who don't let anything get in their way. I mean, I am scared when I play rugby but I like those guys who aren't, the ones that carry on no matter what, they are proper rugby players. Not like me.

Frequent reference to these qualities was made and they often demanded that athletes, particularly those at the elite level, show commitment to the team by playing with pain. Many of the children had a strong sense of what they felt an athlete should look like, how they should act and how they should respond to injury and painful experiences.

> Tom: Well, you can't be fat and eat loads of rubbish. You have to train loads, at the start I don't think you have much of a life, but it's worth it when you get really good ... You have to train to get good, strong muscles and warm-up so you don't get injured. If you do, you have to be tough and not let it stop you reaching your goals.

The images described by the children have a marked relationship to Hughes and Coakley's 'sports ethic' (1991) indicating that the children may use criteria similar to the 'sports ethic' to act as a means to judge both theirs and others' behaviour.

Culture of Risk versus Culture of Precaution: Active Negotiations

It would be imprudent to assume that the 'culture of risk' constitutes a straightforward, wholly unchallenged and all-consuming acceptance of risk, normalisation of injury and glorification of pain in all levels of sport. The cultural context of sports participation may actually be more complex than Nixon's (1993) 'culture of risk' implies. Whilst a number of ethnographic studies substantiate Nixon's (1994) claims that there is a widespread acceptance of pain and injury in competitive sport, they also uncover the complex ways in which those within sporting figurations (re)produce, respond and interact with this culture (Roderick et al. 2000; Malcolm and Sheard 2002; Safai 2003).

Nixon (1994) presents the role of the athlete within the 'sportsnet' as relatively powerless and asserts that athletes are led to conclude that playing though pain is their only viable option should they wish to continue. Moreover, he argues that 'athletes may find it difficult to escape the hold of the culture of risk and related structural influences unless they receive strong support from people outside the sports establishment' (Nixon 1993, 190). Contemporary research challenges Nixon's model and suggests that a 'culture of precaution', which tempers the influence of the dominant 'culture of risk', may exist within sporting environments (Safai 2003).

Safai's model indicates that clinicians and coaches do not subscribe heavily to stereotypical behaviours of masking, denying or downplaying pain and injury but rather, they are involved in 'interpersonal negotiation' with the athletes leading to the emergence of what Safai (2003, 135) terms a 'culture of precaution'. The mediators of a 'culture of precaution' around the children predominately took the form of doctors, physiotherapists, coaches and parents, particularly the mothers of rugby-playing boys. Many of the children spoke of their coaches exercising caution if a member of the team appeared in pain or to be suffering from an injury.

> Eddie: When it [torn back muscle] happened I carried on playing, I wanted to play, it felt awful. My coach saw I was in pain and took me off. I carried on 'cause of the adrenalin rush, I don't want to back out of it. When he took me off I was miserable 'cause I thought I could keep going but afterwards I could see why he had taken me off. I couldn't really run [laughs] and I couldn't even bend down and that is kinda important for a prop.

Safai presents the 'sportsnet' as a site of negotiation and communication rather than a 'conspiratorial alliance of coaches, athletic administrators, sports medicine personnel and others' (Walk 1997, 23). In so doing, she asserts that athletes have access to various power sources and are able to exercise this power through the active negotiation of their treatment. In line with Safai's conclusions the interview data also suggested that the children in the sample actively contested the decisions and recommendations of other members of the sportsnet. Doctors' recommendations were frequently ignored or adapted and attempts were made to mask pain or injuries from significant others. Such behaviour was particularly noticeable if the recommendations did not conform to the wishes of the child in question. For example, Jessica, spoke of her response to her doctor's recommendations:

> I had hurt my knee playing hockey, this big girl had tackled me and I fell over, my knee kinda twisted, I guess I fell funny, it really hurt and got really big. But I carried on 'cause we were winning and I didn't want to come off. The next day, I couldn't really walk, my knee was huge and really sore , so mum made me go to the doctor. The doctor told me I

had to rest for three weeks and not do any sport. But I played the match next day, mum would be mad if she knew, I just told her I was going to watch.

The children emphasised their desire to take control of decisions related to their body 'if I am injured, it should be my choice whether I play on, not my mum's or the coach's, only I know how much pain I am in and only I know my limits' (Katherine). Both the boys and girls interviewed stressed the ownership of their own bodies. In many cases they linked increased injury rates to their *individual, personal* failure to warm-up appropriately, whilst simultaneously highlighting their wish to be in control of decisions related to their continued bodily activities. On occasions where others enforced their decision upon the injured child, emotions such as resentment, frustration and questioned judgement were reported.

'You wuss, get up and stop acting like a girl': Risk in Sport and the Construction of Gendered Identities

A plethora of literature exists which links the rationalisation of risk with dominant masculine subcultures in sport (Messner and Sabo 1990; Young et al. 1994; White and Young 1997; Dunning 1999).[3] It has been argued that 'masculine sport subcultures foster and encourage an unquestioned acceptance of risk and injury' and that the 'tolerance of risk is understood to be valued by many male athletes as masculinising' (Young et al. 1994, 176). Equally it has been suggested that sportsmen utilise the acceptance of risk, tolerance of injury and normalisation of pain as a means of constructing and maintaining their masculine identity, their status as a player and establishing their social position within a team (Colburn 1985).

Young et al. (1994, 177) assert that 'tolerance of physical risk carries enormous symbolic weight in the exhibition and evaluation of masculinity' whereby it is common that a 'willingness to risk injury is at least as highly valued as the demonstration of pure skill'. Those male athletes who did not tolerate pain and failed to play through their injuries were routinely ridiculed and their sporting efforts trivialised (Young et al. 1994). Furthermore those athletes who demonstrate pain had the nature of their sexuality questioned and they 'run the risk of being stigmatized by peers as less than fully masculine, particularly if the injury is not perceived as serious' (Young et al. 1994, 190).

In light of the strong evidence which suggests there are particular cultural and social pressures on male athletes to express a specific masculine identity through sport, to which stoic tolerance of pain is an integral part, a number of academics have examined female athletes' perceptions of, and relationships with, risk, pain and injury in sport (Young and White 1995; Pike and Maguire 2003; Charlesworth and Young 2004). Where previous studies implicitly inferred that the tolerance of pain;

---

3 Also see Merryweather in this volume for a discussion of the discursive relationship between masculinity and risk.

the normalisation of injury; and the unquestioned acceptance of physical risk were the sole preserves of male athletes, these studies uncovered substantial evidence to suggest that 'risk-taking in women's sport bears some similarities to the trends found in men's sport (Pike and Maguire 2003, 243). However, Pike and Maguire (2003) are swift to highlight the complexities and intricacies of the females' relationship with pain, attitudes to injury and acceptance of risk. They argue that one cannot explain the observed similarities with the charge that the women are merely taking on masculine norms and exhibiting masculine behaviours. But rather, the women are actively and consciously negotiating their gendered identity.

Both the qualitative and quantitative data generated by this study revealed few notable gender differences in the children's perception of risk within a sporting environment or social response to sporting related pain and injury. Whilst further research is definitely required in this area, early indications concur with Charlesworth and Young's (2004, 178) conclusion that pain and injury experiences may be a 'product of socialisation into sport culture per se' rather than placing an emphasis on gender socialisation.

Concluding Thoughts

While there exists a substantial body of sociological literature dedicated to the risk, pain and injury experiences of adult sports performers we can observe that children's everyday lived experiences of risk, pain and injury have been largely ignored (Young 2004). The data presented in this chapter begins efforts to address this disparity in research and brings to the fore a number of issues related to children's conceptualisation and lived experiences of 'risk' and the role sport plays in these processes.

The data challenges existing conceptualisations of sports-related risk and highlights the ways in which young people variously understand and relate to 'risk' in differing contexts. The data highlighted the plurality of sports-related risks, drawing particular attention to a social dimension that has previously been under-represented in research. Children appeared to 'trade-off' risks involving their body against the risk of damage to their social identities. This was particularly evident with children at the higher end of the participation spectrum, that is, those who had high personal investment in their athletic identity.

Furthermore, sport appears to provide a context wherein constructions of risk differ to those which are typically bound up with moral panic. In contrast to the construction of risk observed within the current moral panic surrounding 'obesity' (see Gard and Wright, 2005; Rich and Evans 2005), sport-related risk appears immune to calls for individual control, management and self-regulation. Viewed as episodes of 'bad luck' or under the control of external factors, sports-related risk is considered merely an unavoidable part of 'the game'. It would appear then, that 'risk' is social and culturally constructed in distinct ways within the context of sport. Further research is required to understand the complexities of these often contradictory discourses.

Moreover, the data highlights broader issues connecting with children's rights. As illustrated, children's participation in sport incorporates the involvement of a number of key agents who have an investment in either the child, or their performance. Children's relationship with risk is bound up in active and complex negotiations with parents, medical staff and teachers over the child's risk, pain and injury experiences. This raises a number of ethical questions and stimulates significant debate about the role children in decision-making processes related to *their* bodies and their health more broadly (see Freeman 1983; 1998). Beyond the scope of this chapter, these issues require significant attention and may have considerable implications for Physical Education, Sport and Health policies.

References

Charlesworth, H. and Young, K. (2004), 'Why English Female University Athletes Play with Pain', in Young, K. (ed.) (2004), *Sporting Bodies, Damaged Selves: Sociological Studies of Sports-Related Injury* (Oxford: Elsevier Science Press).

Coakley, J. (1998), *Sport in Society: Issues and Controversies*, 6th Edition (Mosley: Irwin McGraw Hill).

Coakley, J. (2003), *Sport in Society: Issues and Controversies*, International Edition (Mosley: Irwin McGraw Hill).

Colburn, K. (1985), 'Honour, Ritual and Violence in Ice Hockey', *Canadian Journal of Sociology* 1:2, 153–70.

Connell, R. (1990), 'An Iron Man: The Body and Some Contradictions of Hegemonic Masculinity', in Messner, M. and Sabo, D. (eds.) (1990), *Sport, Men and the Gender Order* (Champaign, Illinois: Human Kinetics).

Curry, T. (1993), 'A Little Pain Never Hurt Anyone: Athletic Career Socialization and the Normalization of Sports Injury', *Symbolic Interaction* 16:3, 273–90.

Curry, T. and Strauss, R. (1994), 'A Little Pain Never Hurt Anybody: A Photo-essay on the Normalisation of Sports Injury', *Sociology of Sport Journal* 11, 195–208.

Department of Health (2005), *Choosing Activity: A Physical Activity Action Plan* (London: Department of Health/ National Health Service Publications).

Dunning, E. (1999), *Sport Matters* (London: Routledge).

Elias, N. (2000), *The Civilizing Process* (Oxford, Blackwell).

Evans, J. et al. (2003), 'The Only Problem Is, Children Will Like Their Chips: Education and the Discursive Production of Ill-Health', *Pedagogy, Culture and Society* 11:2, 215–40.

Ewald, K. and Jiobu, R. (1985), 'Explaining Positive Deviance: Becker's Model and the Case of Runners and Bodybuilders', *Sociology of Sport Journal* 8:144–56.

Flintoff, A. (2005), *Being Freddie: My Story so Far* (London: Hodder and Stoughton).

Freeman, M. (1983), *The Rights and Wrongs of Children* (London: Pinter).

Freeman, M. (1998), 'The Sociology of Childhood and Children's Right', *The International Journal of Children's Rights* 6:4, 433–44.

Gard, M. and Wright, J. (2005), *The Obesity Epidemic: Science, Morality and Ideology* (London: Routledge).

Greig, A. and Taylor, J. (1999), *Doing Research with Children* (London, Sage)

Howe, P. D. (2004), *Sport, Professionalism and Pain: Ethnographies of Injury and Risk* (London: Routledge).

Hughes, R. and Coakley, J. (1991), 'Positive Deviance Among Athletes: The Implications of Overconformity to the Sports Ethic', *Sociology of Sport Journal* 8:307–25.

Loland, S. et al. (2006), *Pain and Injury in Sport: Social and Ethical Analysis* (London: Routledge).

Malcolm, D. and Sheard, K. (2002). 'Pain in the Assets: The Effects of Commercialisation and Professionalisation on the Management of Injury in English Rugby Union', *Sociology of Sport Journal* 19:2, 149–69.

May, T. (2001), *Social Research: Issues, Methods & Process*, 3rd Edition (Buckingham: Open University Press).

Mennell, S. and Goudsblom, J. (1998), *Norbert Elias on Civilization, Power and Knowledge* (Chicago: University of Chicago Press).

Messner, M. and Sabo, D. (eds.) (1990), *Sport, Men and the Gender Order* (Champaign, Illinois: Human Kinetics).

Morris, D. (1991), *The Culture of Pain* (Berkeley: University of California Press).

National Audit Office (2005), 'Improving School Attendance in England (London: The Stationery Office).

Nixon, H.L. (1993), 'Accepting the Risks of Pain and Injury in Sport: Mediated Cultural Influences on Playing Hurt', *Sociology of Sport Journal* 10:183–96.

—— (1994), 'Coaches Views of Risk, Pain and Injury in Sport: With Special Reference To Gender Differences', *Sociology of Sport Journal* 11:79–87.

—— (1996), 'Explaining Pain and Injury Attitudes and Experiences in Sport in terms of Gender, Race and Sports Status Factors', *Journal of Sport and Social Issues* 21:33–45.

Pike, E. and Maguire, J. (2003), 'Injury in Women's Sport: Classifying Key Elements of "Risk Encounters"', *Sociology of Sport Journal* 20:232–51.

Rich, E. and Evans, J. (2005), 'Fat Ethics: The Obesity Discourse and Body Politics', *Social Theory & Health* 3:4, 341–58.

Roderick, M. et al. (2000), 'Playing Hurt: Managing Injuries in English Professional Football', *International Review for the Sociology of Sport* 35:2, 165–80.

Safai, P. (2003), 'Healing The Body in the "Culture of Risk": Examining the Negotiation of Treatment Between Sport Medicine Clinicians and Injured Athletes in Canadian Intercollegiate Sport', *Sociology of Sport Journal* 20:127–46.

Sport England (2005), 'The Value of Sport', [website], (updated 19 August 2005) <http://www.sportengland.org/index/get_resources/vosm.html>

Van Krieken, R. (1998), *Norbert Elias* (London: Routledge).

Walk, S. (1997), 'Peers in Pain: The Experiences of Student Athlete Trainers', *Sociology of Sport Journal* 14:22–56.

White, P. and Young, K. (1997), 'Masculinity, Sport and the Injury Process: A Review of Canadian and International Evidence', *Avante* 3:1–30.

Young, K. et al. (1994), 'Body Talk: Male Athletes Reflect on Sport, Injury and Pain', *Sociology of Sport Journal* 11:175–94.

Young, K. (ed.) (2004), *Sporting Bodies, Damaged Selves: Sociological Studies of Sports-Related Injury* (Oxford: Elsevier Science Press).

Young, K. and White, P. (1995), 'Sport, Physical Danger and Injury: The Experience of Elite Women Athletes', *Journal of Sport and Social Issues* 19:1, 45–61.

Chapter 5

Talking Risks: Constructing Desired Masculinities

Dave Merryweather

Introduction

Conventional accounts of risk are often accompanied by an emphasis on processes of individualisation and detraditionalisation. When applied to the relationship between risk and gender such concepts tend to suggest that something of a 'levelling-out' process is occurring whereby men and women are engaging in various risk-behaviours on a more-or-less equal basis. However, this is to simplify matters considerably. Not only do risks remain distributed according to more traditional social cleavages, but there also remains a strong sense in which risk-discourses are heavily gendered. Indeed, risk-discourses are often articulated with gender discourses in ways that produce particular configurations of the gendered subject (Green and Singleton 2006). Moreover, while exploring the links between risk-taking and gendered identity is not entirely new, such accounts have tended to focus almost exclusively on the material practices of risk-behaviours, ignoring the crucial role occupied by discursive practices and strategies.

The aim of this chapter is to develop an account of risk and gender which takes into account the broader discursive practices *in* and *through* which gendered identities are constituted. By analysing focus-group data I argue that, not only do young males routinely encounter and practise a range of risk-activities but, that *in* and *through* their conversations about risk (what I refer to here as 'risk-talk'), they practise particular technologies of the self (Foucault 1985), constructing and re-constructing their masculine identities. Utilising insights from poststructural thought I illustrate the extent to which 'risk-talk' cannot only be conceptualised as part of the broader discursive process of subject-positioning, but also how such talk reveals the endlessly deferred, malleable and problematic character of gendered identity. Indeed, in exploring such issues, I suggest that paying attention to discursive practices helps grasp the fluid and uncertain character of masculinities in a way that accounts informed by hegemonic masculinity so often aspire to, but frequently fail to achieve.

Youth, Risk and Gender

Arguably, a major development in youth-lifestyles in recent years has been the apparent convergence of young men and women's risk-taking behaviours. While males continue to lead the way with regard to a broad range of risk-taking behaviours such as excessive alcohol-consumption, violent crime and unprotected sex; statistical evidence suggests that women are beginning to close this gap. To illustrate briefly, recent Government statistics regarding patterns of alcohol consumption indicate that while men continue to drink more than women the gap is narrowing. In 1998 thirty-nine per cent of males consumed eight units or more on at least one day in the week prior to interview. By 2002 however, this had fallen to thirty-four per cent. By contrast, during the same period the figures for 16–24 year-old women increased with the proportion drinking six units or more rising from twenty-four per cent to twenty-eight per cent. Indeed, reflecting a more general increase in alcohol consumption amongst women, by 2002 some thirty-three per cent of 16–24 year olds in England and Wales were reported to be consuming more than fourteen units a week compared with just twenty-two per cent in 1997 (Office for National Statistics 2005). Likewise official statistics indicate that although men remain more likely than women to be the main perpetrators of violent crime again this gap is showing signs of narrowing. During the period 2002/04 in England and Wales, women were involved in twenty-one per cent of violent incidents, mainly against other women as compared to eighteen per cent in 1996/98 (Hough et al. 2005). At one level of analysis such trends may be read as evidence of the wider processes of 'detraditionalisation' and 'individualisation' (Beck 1992; Giddens 1991) inasmuch as, freed from the traditional constraints of gender young women are engaging in particular risk-activities which have historically been associated with men and masculinity. Genuine concerns regarding the potential damage associated with these risks aside, such activities could be read as libratory acts which are functioning to undo gender. However, this is to over-simplify matters considerably. On the one hand, while various risk factors may be experienced and negotiated at an individual level their actual social distribution still remains structured largely by traditional factors such as gender and class (Margo et al. 2006; Furlong and Cartmel 2007). Moreover, such an interpretation elides the fact that many risk-taking behaviours remain intrinsically bound-up with gendered discourses. For example, not only has recent empirical work argued that young women's risk-taking and risk-related behaviour is still shaped by cultural notions of female respectability (Green and Singleton 2006), recent literatures exploring hegemonic masculinity (Connell 1987; 2000) have illustrated how a gender position is constructed around traits such as independence, assertiveness, toughness and heterosexuality, with the understanding that these are attributes that males seek to assert via their engagement in certain risk-taking practices (Messerschmidt 1994; Canaan 1996). Killick, in this volume, clearly relates 'toughness', risk uptake and injury as important 'masculinizing' processes in the social world of elite athletes. Elsewhere, there is a strong sense in which risk-activities such as alcohol consumption and violence continue to be read as suggestive of certain masculine identity positions (Archer 1994; Stoudt 2006).

In considering this relationship between risk and gender, the overwhelming tendency has been to focus on the material practices of risk-taking. Important though such practices undoubtedly are the focus here is to consider the extent to which particular risks are immanently connected with gendered discourses in general and discourses of masculinity in particular. This entails positing risks as discursive constructs which are themselves imbued with a whole series of value-laden meanings and cultural assumptions regarding what is defined as risk, and how individuals should act in relation to these (Tulloch and Lupton 2003). Such a discursive approach enables risks to be read as discourses which are in circulation alongside numerous other discourses and which simultaneously position, and are taken-up or resisted by, individuals as part of a broader process of establishing subjectivity (Hall 1992). Read thus, developing an adequate understanding of the relationship between risk and gender entails going beyond a simple analysis of statistical trends and an examination of the material practices of risk-taking. Rather, attention must focus also on how risk-discourses are articulated with other discourses in ways that operate to construct and organise gender relations by reaffirming old, and producing new, gender divisions and hierarchies (Adkins 2002).

Such an analysis itself rests on a conceptualisation of the gendered subject as a discursive construct, constituted in flows of language and meaning, inherently fragmented, contradictory and fluid, and dependent upon specific articulations of discourses within particular cultural and historical contexts (Hall 1990; Foucault 1985; Butler 1989). Such a poststructural position simultaneously avoids the tendency in much hegemonic masculinity literature to imply a relatively fixed and static model of gender in which hegemonic and subordinated masculinities are constructed as clearly differentiated configurations of practice; each characterised by a definable, distinctive essence (Demetriou 2001; Petersen 2003), and encapsulates something of the fluidity and malleability of gender, acknowledging that the organised forms of intelligibility which make up the 'hegemonic' in any particular context are multiple, varied and deeply complex (Wetherell and Edley 1999, 30). This suggests that what constitutes the 'hegemonic' is best understood merely as another gender discourse; the character and meanings of which are dependent on context and who is speaking (Cornwall and Lindisfarne 1994).

Given the unstable and contingent character of gendered identities that this implies it is necessary for individuals to cite various discourses and employ particular strategies by way of seeking to position themselves as stable, 'authentic', individuals. As Whitehead (2002) puts it: 'for man to be and become that very category of being requires, then, constant engagement in those discursive practices of signification that suggest masculinity (2002, 212). In this respect it is thus perhaps more useful to talk of *desired* rather than hegemonic masculinity. As Whitehead further suggests, this desire *to be* in the social world is played out in particular social and cultural contexts in which what constitutes the 'desired masculinity' is represented in different ways. Motivated by desire, male subjects practice a range of technologies of the self in an endless quest to identify with what is only ever a temporary, and ultimately elusive, masculine ideal. The concept of 'desired masculinity' thus begins to grasp the ephemeral character of masculinity, drawing attention to its immanent instability and fluidity, and providing a more productive understanding of the many apparent tensions and contradictions in men's identities as they seek to position themselves in the subject positions that are made available.

Given that cultural perceptions of, and responses to, risk continue to be gendered (Tulloch and Lupton 2003) it is apparent that those 'discursive practices suggestive of masculinity' must inevitably include risk discourses also. As such, an adequate account of gendered identity must consider both the ways in which individuals position themselves and others vis-à-vis risk discourses and how these are routinely articulated with gendered discourses in effecting particular conceptualisations of the masculine subject. This entails consideration of how individuals position themselves and others in risk and gender discourses through context-specific 'risk-talk'.

Analysing 'Risk-Talk'

The relationship between 'risk-talk' and the discursive construction of masculine identities is explored here via consideration of data generated in a pilot focus-group conducted as part of a broader research project examining the relationships between risk and young people's lifestyles. This group consisted of six, fifteen year-old males drawn from a comprehensive school in North-west England and was internally homologous along lines of socio-economic classification and ethnicity. The purpose of the focus-group was to facilitate discussion of the various activities regarded as 'risky' and which were considered to be typical of their everyday lives. Questions were designed according to the principles of Hollway and Jefferson's (2000) 'biographical-interpretivist' method so as to encourage participants to narrativise accounts of 'risk' in their own terms and from within their own meaning frames. Such an approach was regarded here as being most useful in eliciting responses which constitute a more accurate account of the relation of certain risk-taking behaviours to participants' identities in the context of their respective everyday lives.

The group's 'risk-talk' was subsequently subjected to a discourse analysis with specific attention focused on aspects which could be read as exemplar of the discursive practices *in* and *through* which participants position themselves as men whose gender corresponds with a contextually-specific desired masculinity. This implies that in the course of their 'risk-talk participants were continuously positioning both themselves and others within the contextually-specific discourses, including those of risk and gender, which were in circulation (Davies and Harrè 1990). That is to say, the conversational interactions occurring within the focus group were viewed not as benign, neutral, accounts of reality, but as based around various interpretive repertoires; 'the culturally familiar and habitual lines of argument which include recognizable themes, common places and tropes' (Wetherell 1998, 400) which are informed by discourses and which permit what is knowable and organise our knowledge and understanding of the social world and concepts of self (Davies and Harrè 1990; Wetherell and Edley 1999). The 'risk-talk' generated in the course of the focus group was thus read as constituting various 'technologies of the self' (Foucault 1985) *in* and *through* which individuals position themselves in the subject-positions made available by contextually-specific discourses. Such an approach entails paying close attention to the various interpretive repertoires, including linguistic repertoires (Woolfit 1993) and rhetorical devices manifest in 'risk-talk', which are illustrative of those strategies employed by individuals by way of seeking to construct their gendered identities in particular terms. This in turn entails both consideration of how individuals seek to fix their gendered identities, and recognition that such positioning is never complete, as Davies and Harrè (1990, 3) suggest:

> An individual emerges through the processes of social interaction, not as a relatively fixed end product, but as one who is constituted and reconstituted through the various discursive practices in which they participate. Accordingly, who one is always an open question with a shifting answer depending upon the positions made available within one's own and other's discursive practices, the stories through which we make sense of our own and others' lives.

Indeed, analysis of 'risk-talk' as discussed here reveals not only the various attempts at 'fixing' gendered identity, but also the unstable and fluid character of gender as illustrated by the numerous shifts, inconsistencies and contradictions in the form of the desired masculinity that is materialised throughout their conversations.

Talking Risks: Constructing Masculinities

During the course of focus group discussions the two groups of young males identified a range of activities or places regarded as the main 'risks' characteristic of their everyday lives. These included fighting with other youths; alcohol consumption; sexual encounters; drug-use; smoking; night-clubs; and certain 'risk areas' such as particular districts, the city-centre and alleyways. 'Risk-talk' regarding these issues explicates the gendered character of risk discourses and the discursive processes *in* and *through* which they seek to position both themselves and others in particular gendered positions. Indeed, not only does analysis reveal the ways in which young males seek to position themselves in accordance with a contextually-specific desired masculinity, it also draws attention to the fluid and inherently problematic and unstable character of such gender positions.

By way of exemplifying these processes I focus on 'risk-talk' as it specifically relates to fighting with other youths, alcohol consumption and attitudes towards sexual relationships. While not presented as an everyday occurrence there was a general expectation that fights with other youths could ensue at anytime and anywhere and in this regard such a threat constituted a reasonably high source of anxiety amongst participants. Sex was also not an everyday risk in that only two participants had actually experienced sexual intercourse. Nevertheless there was recognition that sexual activity entailed a range of risks. By contrast, alcohol consumption was regarded as a significant risk-activity typical of participants' everyday lifestyles; all claiming to have been regular drinkers since about the age of thirteen and now drinking routinely at weekends. Much of the talk regarding these issues suggested that concern was directed less at the potential damage to one's health that such risks posed and more to do with the necessity of practising such behaviours in a manner that would contribute to ensuring the maintenance of a status concomitant with a contextually-specific desired masculinity. In this regard, 'risk-talk' around these issues demonstrates how it is *in* and *through* their conversational interactions that participants position themselves as men of a particular type, establishing boundaries between less desirable forms of masculinity and femininity, and yet simultaneously problematising those very forms of desired masculinity that they construct.

Fighting Talk

'Risk-talk' relating to fighting elucidates both how participants seek to construct themselves as men of a particular type within the conversational context itself and how such talk is informed by broader gender discourses in which values of assertiveness, toughness and bravery constitute signifiers of a contextually-contingent desired masculinity. Drawing on such discourses fighting was posited as a risk-activity that should not be unnecessarily avoided less one wishes to risk having one's status as a 'proper man' undermined. Of particular interest here is the manner in which 'rank' or status was deployed as a discursive mechanism through which the boundaries of a desired masculinity were constructed. This point is illustrated with reference to discussion of the pressures faced in trying to avoid fights. As Steve noted in discussing the difficulties faced in such circumstances, 'but people think it's easy, just saying' 'here you are, just walk away, don't say nothing' but it's not, you think it is but it's just not is it!' This was supported by Paul who noted that in walking away from a fight: 'You lose respect!' This suggests that in striving to maintain a certain masculinity the 'fight' is a risk-activity that once initiated, has to be seen through to the end, regardless of its material consequences. Moreover, in presenting themselves as men who will not walk away from a fight, participants effectively position themselves in a gender discourse that equates desired masculinity with such aggressive behaviour. The implication here is that failure to comply results in a failure to position oneself successfully as a man who corresponds with this notion of masculinity.

'Risk-talk' also reveals the way in which those gender discourses that inform conversations compel young men to position themselves vis-à-vis women and 'femininity'. Speaking of the pressures regarding being viewed as a 'tough male'; Paul's comment below was made concerning the presence of young females in situations in which fights occur:

> Or maybe if girls or what, if girls are there you don't want to like, look like a coward or something' in front of girls do you? ... You want to impress them!'

Here the gendered aspect of this risk-activity is such that doing one's masculinity 'correctly', and thereby appearing as a 'man' to both other males and women, entails certain performances, including standing-up to threatening others, defending oneself, avoiding outward displays of fear and appearing tough in front of women. The successful performance ensures that those punishments meted out to those who fail to do their gender right (Butler 1993) are avoided with one's masculine status being successfully maintained, and a clear distinction from the feminine 'other' being achieved. Indeed, in this context 'risk-talk' can be read as *disciplinary* in that various linguistic repertoires such as *'respect'* and *'coward'* ensure that participants police each other and themselves by way of seeking identification with the desired masculinity.

Furthermore, there is also a suggestion that such positioning is contextually-contingent and that while participants may seek identification with a particular masculinity in one situation, this is not always necessarily so with the performances required in identifying with the desired masculinity varying according to context. To exemplify, while repeatedly indicating that fights were *not* to be avoided, it was also suggested that there were certain circumstances in which they would *not* fight, particularly where this involved certain groups such as notorious families/gangs, police officers and nightclub doormen. Hence:

> Paul: You also don't mess with like [mentions family name] – you try to stay out of fights with tough families, like say a family has got a name for themselves, and they do something to you, you try to just let it go!

Such comments are illustrative of the discursive mechanisms deployed by way of delineating the symbolic boundaries of their masculinity; a boundary that should not be transgressed less they evoke either actual or symbolic harm to their masculine status. In this regard, fighting with certain gangs was constructed as too dangerous. However, rather than constituting a 'failure' to position oneself in terms of a desired masculinity the discursive strategies deployed actually serve to position them more securely within a specific masculine position. In justifying their reasons for avoiding such encounters for example, Steve noted that:

> Steve: ... it's not like you are scared or anything, it's like you don't want a fight because that's what they're like ... You don't want to fight with the wrong person, not because you're scared, you'll fight on the day but (..) you'll see them come up day-after-day-after-day fighting with you till you're dead basically.

The word 'scared' functions here as a symbolic marker which delineates the limits of the desired masculinity in that to be scared, or even to be *seen* to be scared, is constructed as the point at which one may fail to position oneself in accordance with the discourse of the desired position. However, in repudiating the notion that he may be 'scared' of certain gangs and in asserting that he would '*fight on the day*', Steve continues to position himself in accordance with within the discourses of a desired masculinity. Moreover, the form that this masculinity takes has now been modified, having now been supplemented with additional qualities such as the ability to make rational, calculative, evaluations as to the merits of particular conflicts.

The suggestion that the characteristics of desired masculinity is contextually-specific is further illustrated when considering the discussion of the form that certain fights may take. In the following extract Alan discusses a hypothetical fight involving a knife attack by another youth:

Alan: I'd probably get the knife and just lash it – If I was to, if he got up and throwed [sic] the knife I'd go over and find the knife and run over and stab him to death (.) but (.) saying that I wouldn't (..) I couldn't stab somebody to death. People say you're living with it for life, for killing someone is just horrible.

At first glance the speaker appears to be positioning himself as an aggressive, violent male who corresponds with particular configurations of the desired ideal. However, again the limits of such a position are delineated inasmuch as the extreme claims of the first part of the statement are mitigated by the second part in which the speaker's utterances position him as a particular moral being. In this regard therefore, the specific 'technologies of the self' practised *in* and *through* 'risk-talk' constitute the discursive construction of a particular ethical subject (Foucault 1985) in which the symbolic boundaries of this position are clearly established. But moreover, the sudden disjuncture in Alan's 'risk-talk constitutes a discursive repositioning, underlining Davies and Harrè's (1990) point that who one is; is always an open question.

Consequently, analysis of 'risk-talk' regarding fighting may be read as illustrating a number of discursive processes *in* and *through* which participants position themselves as men of a certain type. However, the precise form that these conversations take, and thereby the form that desired masculinity takes, varies considerably according to context and who is speaking.

'Real men drink beer'

As with fighting, while there was a material reality to practices relating to alcohol consumption with participants claiming to consume regularly a range of strong beers and spirits, the actual risk-discourses cited and reiterated in 'risk-talk' could clearly be read as gendered and as such warrants further consideration. 'Risk-talk' pertaining to alcohol consumption contributed to discursive processes of positioning within specific discourses of masculinity. For example, in describing the drinks most regularly consumed a range of linguistic repertoires were employed by way of distinguishing between 'masculine' and 'feminine' drinks. Beverages such as Lambrini, Reef, Smirnoff Ice, and Bacardi Breezer were identified clearly as 'girls' and 'birds' drinks, being posited in distinctly 'feminine' terms as being 'easy to drink', containing 'only five per cent alcohol', 'tasting like juice' and as coming in 'light coloured bottles'. While such terminology may be read as a series of benign categorising devices I would suggest that they are perhaps better understood as examples of those 'extreme case formulations' and 'linguistic repertoires' (Woolfit 1993) deployed by way of influencing the attitudes and opinions of co-interactants and which serve to simultaneously normalise and abnormalise certain activities. Viewed thus, defining these beverages in such terms may be read as illustrative of the citation and reiteration of gender discourses that posit some deep-seated, 'natural' dichotomy between men and women, a discourse that constructs women as 'improper drinkers' who prefer weaker, brightly coloured, drinks and, by extension, rendering 'abnormal' the consumption of such drinks by 'real' men. The discursive effect of such terms is clearly disciplinary, serving to bring the behaviour and attitudes of participants into line with the normative conventions of gender discourses.

Such disciplinary repertoires were evident throughout participants' 'risk-talk' as was further evidenced by the various linguistic injunctions deployed by way of constructing and policing the boundaries of their masculinity. For example, in discussing the pressures to consume 'appropriate' brands of alcohol Robbie noted that being seen consuming 'feminine' drinks could result in an oral reprimand from peers to the effect of: 'eeee! Why are you drinking that? you're a girl! It's a bird's drink!'. Or being condemned as 'a light drinker' who is 'not experienced'. Developing the point, Robbie further noted that to be viewed consuming such drinks by girls could result in being referred to as 'gay' or as 'not very masculine', adding that:

> Robbie: ... you're trying to, to get your rank, to look (.) you're trying to make you look hard, you're trying to look tough aren't you (.) you don't want to be drinking a *girls'* drink.

Not only was masculinity linked discursively to the consumption of appropriate brands of alcohol, there was also clear emphasis on the necessity of consuming, or moreover, being seen to have consumed, certain levels of alcohol. As Robbie suggested, 'if you go out for the night or a sit-off and you drink say three bottles – you're not going to be seen as a drinker are you'.[1]

In a similar vein Carl suggested that:

> if people say how many bottles do you get drunk on and you say 'four' they're like 'aaaahhh' [mocking tone]. You think better of people (.) because you're like, if you don't (..) say like on three pints I got bevied [drunk] they're like 'he's a light drinker, he can't

---

1   A *'sit-off'* is the colloquial term for gathering together for the purposes of socializing, usually involving consumption if alcohol.

drink' but if I say I've had seven pints and I'm only a little bit bevied it's like wow! he *can* drink!

In this regard, analysis of 'risk-talk' suggests that successful identification with a specific masculinity entails certain risk-behaviours – both material and discursive – which convey the impression of being able to consume the levels of alcohol appropriate to the desired masculinity. Moreover, again the limits of this position are policed through the deployment of specific discursive resources; terms such as 'girl', 'bird', 'a light drinker', 'gay' and 'not very masculine' constituting symbolic boundaries. In this regard, deployment of particular linguistic repertoires is an exemplar of the citation and reiteration of dominant gender-discourses which position 'femininity' and 'homosexuality' as inferior vis-à-vis a desired masculinity which is simultaneously inscribed exclusively in heterosexual terms.

However, again it is important to recognise that desired masculinity is not fixed but varies according to context and who is speaking. Indeed, their 'risk-talk' illustrates the extent to which positioning is an ongoing, endlessly deferred process in which 'who one is'; is continuously being revised. Consequently, different versions of the masculine subject are brought into effect according to the different permutations of discourses that prevail in any given conversational moment. This was clearly evident whereby it was recognised that what constitutes risk in one context may not do so in another. For example, it was suggested that certain drinks consumed as younger teenagers were no longer deemed appropriate to fifteen-year-old males. Hence, while 'cider' was regarded as sufficiently 'risky' to signify a particular masculine identity when aged thirteen to fourteen years old; this was no longer considered to be the case with a range of much stronger beers and spirits now being posited as 'men's' drinks.

Moreover, further analysis highlights how processes of gendering are never quite carried out according to expectation, with participants not always and consistently inhabiting the masculine ideal they are compelled to approximate (Butler 1993). Thus, while noting that certain drinks should be avoided due to their 'feminine' qualities, it was later noted that they actually enjoyed such drinks. For example, Carl stated quite emphatically that: 'I like girls' drinks! ... Yeah, I like girls' drinks 'cos they've got vodka in them', while Rob claimed that '... Lambrini is a nice drink ....' The corollary of this is that while gender discourses inform what is permissible and non-permissible this is by no means fixed. Indeed, the very presence of those linguistic repertoires utilised by way of policing the boundaries of gendered identity are illustrative of this, for if such binaries were 'natural' there would be no need to keep them under surveillance. Nevertheless, the mere fact of the groups' consumption of 'girls' drinks' clearly highlights the malleable, fluid and constructed character of these gender binaries. Indeed, it can quite readily be claimed that such acts may be read as a form of 'drag', an act of subversion that 'brings into relief what is, after all, determined only in relation to the hyperbolic: the understated, taken-for-granted quality of heterosexual performativity' (Butler 1993, 114).

Talking Sex

As a final example this gendered character of 'risk-talk' was further evident in relation to sex. 'Risk-talk' in this respect alluded to a number of potential 'risks', particularly the threat of material consequences such as unwanted pregnancy and sexually transmitted diseases. Discussions of the pressures from peers to have had sexual intercourse by a certain age may also be regarded as a 'risk' in terms of the potential damage to one's status as a 'real man'. Moreover, 'risk-talk' concerning attitudes towards male and female sexual behaviour were clearly framed within dominant discourses of what is considered 'appropriate' and 'inappropriate' sexual behaviour; illustrating further the gendering of risk discourses and how in specific contexts these operate to normalise heterosexuality and naturalise gender 'differences'.

To exemplify, while most participants had not actually experienced sexual intercourse they nevertheless articulated a perceived pressure to have done so before a certain age. Such a 'pressure' was accounted for on the basis that, as Carl put it: 'everyone wants sex don't they'. The word 'everyone' is read here as an extreme case formulation that serves to normalise sexual behaviour. But more than this, as participants' 'risk-talk' referred only to sex with women, and as terms associated with homosexuality such as 'gay' and 'queer' were deployed elsewhere as negative, disciplinary, sanctions, it follows that the sexual behaviour being normalised was exclusively that of heterosexuality. Furthermore, 'risk-talk' on sex was framed very much within a heavily gendered discourse in which an assertive masculinity was valorised while an assertive female sexuality was denigrated. In this respect, analysis of the linguistic repertoires uttered, elucidates the extent, not only to which dominant gender regimes are cited and reproduced, but how such discourses serve to reproduce power relations between men and women. Hence, there was a clear inference that active sexual behaviour on the part of men is regarded as 'normal' and therefore justifiable. Alan, for example, suggested that men having several sexual partners was 'better' and something to be 'proud of'. While Carl, in claiming that men want sex more, stated that: 'it's just the way it is'. Conversely, the groups' 'risk-talk' tended to posit similar sexual activity by women in negative terms whereby the idea of girls having a number of sexual partners was regarded as 'worse', 'disgusting' and 'horrible' with such behaviour likely to be disciplined through the deployment of negative sanctions such as 'slag' and 'slapper'.

As with the group's categorisation of different alcoholic beverages such linguistic repertoires are again read here as performances that both cite and reiterate the normative conventions of gender – in this case functioning to valorise and normalise an assertive male heterosexuality vis-à-vis other modes of doing gender. The point is underscored by their discussion of the assumed biological basis for differences in male and female sexual behaviour with Robbie accounting for such differences via a reference to 'the hormones', while both Steve and Paul justified male assertive sexual behaviour by claiming simply that 'men need it more, men need it!'. Such 'talk' is again illustrative of those repeated performances that 'congeal over time to produce the appearance of substance, of a natural sort of being' (Butler 1989, 33); that is to say, such utterances both cite and reproduce dominant gender discourses, 'naturalising' differences in sexual behaviour and thereby normalising the power relations existent between them.

At one level therefore, 'risk-talk' regarding sex is constitutive of particular sexual identities. Moreover, further analysis of the 'risk-talk' indicates the discursive mechanisms in and through which these participants position themselves as particular moral and ethical subjects. Taking their comments regarding appropriate male sexual behaviour at face value, for example, could be interpreted as an indication of their identification with a 'male sexual drive' discourse (Hollway 1984). However, while generally expressing rather liberal attitudes towards sexual behaviour, at least regarding what was permissible for men, their 'risk-talk' did fall short of an 'anything goes' attitude. To exemplify, unprotected sex was not only posited as a 'risk', but also those engaging in unprotected sex were effectively viewed as morally inferior. As Alan put it:

> I hate these people who say 'you got this disease! You got this disease!' How hard is it? Did you wear a condom? 'No!' – Did you wear a jonny? 'No!' I mean, how hard is it not to!

In other words, ethical sexual behaviour entails individual men taking responsibility for their own protection. Similarly, in commenting on unwanted pregnancies Carl stated:

> I think it's wrong as well if you don't wear protection, if you got a girl pregnant and she wants to have the baby and you say 'no!' and you walk away and you don't, you know, take responsibility.

In both examples risks are constructed in particular moral terms with excessive, irresponsible, risk-taking and by extension those who engage in such practices, being cast as morally-inferior and beyond the bounds of acceptability. Indeed, such 'talk' is clearly exemplar of those practical acts of self-governance, a disciplinary 'care for the self' *in* and *through* which individuals position themselves as ethical subjects of a particular discursive regime of morality (Foucault 1985).

Consequently, analysis of 'risk-talk' demonstrates how *in* and *through* various discursive practices participants position themselves within a dominant gendered discourse; one in which heterosexuality is normalised and power hierarchies between men and women reinscribed, and in which their version of desired masculinity is marked by a particular ethical substance.

Concluding Remarks

Analysis of 'risk-talk' around particular risk-activities illustrates the extent to which these are routinely posited as signifiers of masculinity, one marked by assertiveness, aggression, hardness and heterosexuality; characteristics that clearly resonate with conventional conceptualisations of hegemonic masculinity. However, although hegemonic masculinity theory implies fluidity, multiplicity and difference there remains a tendency to posit masculinities as more-or-less de facto categories which men move between, in accomplishing their identity. By contrast, what I have suggested here in an analysis of 'risk-talk' is the extent to which individuals are 'immanently connected to discourse ... embodied and inculcated through discourse ...' (Whitehead 2002, 105). From this perspective, it is *in* and *through* the citation and reiteration of gender and risk discourses, as manifest in contextually specific conversations, that individuals position themselves as men of a particular sort. This is evidenced by the character of 'risk-talk' which is clearly informed by broader gender discourses and the various discursive devices drawn from interpretive repertoires invoked by way of policing the symbolic boundaries of what may be better understood as a *desired masculinity*. In this respect, conversations about fighting, alcohol consumption and sex are all exemplars of how doing a desired masculinity necessitates the 'forcible citation of a norm' (Butler 1993; one that associates masculinity with specific modes of behaviour, and the avoidance of any activity that might be deemed as 'feminine'.

But more than this, analysis of 'risk-talk' reveals also the highly contingent, fluid and malleable character of both risk and gender, the meanings of which are always deferred, but never complete. Certainly a key theme to emerge was how certain risk-activities were conceptualised quite differently in various situations and at different points in time. Consequently, understanding the relationship between risk-taking and the discursive construction of gender entails recognising that in different contexts the risk-discourses *cited* and *reiterated* shift with the result that certain acts are no longer configured as appropriate signifiers of masculinity and that greater, or at least different, risks may have to be taken in positioning oneself as a man of a particular type. The implications for the discursive construction of identity here are clear, for if performativity is understood as '... that reiterative power of discourse to produce the phenomena that it regulates and constrains' (Butler 1993, 2), but the discourses that are cited and reiterated are constantly in flux, then the character of masculinity which is made available is itself unsettled, fluid and malleable. Viewed thus, variations in the form of masculinity can be understood as illustrative of the ways in which individuals position themselves differently according to the specifics of the context in which their conversations are occurring. As such, analysing 'risk-talk' reveals not only the fluid and contingent character of 'risks', but by extension, the fluid and contingent character of gendered identity itself.

References

Adkins, L. (2002), *Revisions: Gender and Sexuality in Late Modernity* (Buckingham: Open University Press).

Archer, J. (ed.) (1994), *Male Violence* (London: Routledge).

Beck, U. (1992), *Risk Society: Towards a New Modernity* (London: Sage).

Butler, J. (1989), *Gender Trouble: Feminism and the Subversion of Identity* (London: Routledge).

Butler, J. (1993), 'Critically Queer', in Du Gay, P. et al. (eds). (2000), *Identity: A Reader* (London: Sage).

Canaan, J. E. (1996), 'One thing leads to another': Drinking, Fighting and Working Class Masculinities', in Mac an Ghaill, M. (ed.) (1996), *Understanding Masculinities* (Buckingham: Open University Press).

Connell, R. W. (1987), *Gender and Power* (Cambridge: Polity).

Connell, R. W. (2000), *The Men and the Boys* (Cambridge: Polity).

Cornwall, A. and Lindisfarne, N. (eds) (1994), *Dislocating Masculinity: Comparative Ethnographies* (London: Routledge).

Davies, B. and Harrè, R. (1990) 'Positioning: The Discursive Production of Selves', *Journal for the Theory of Social Behaviour* 20, 43–63.

Demetriou, D. Z. (2001), 'Connell's concept of hegemonic masculinity: A critique', *Theory and Society* 30:337–361.

Du Gay, P. et al. (eds). (2000), *Identity: A Reader* (London: Sage).

Foucault, M. (1985), *The History of Sexuality, Vol. 2. The Uses of Pleasure* (London: Penguin).

Furlong, A. and Cartmel, F. (2007), *Young People and Social Change: New Perspectives*. 2nd edition (Buckingham: Open University Press).

Giddens, A. (1991), *Modernity and Self-identity* (Cambridge: Polity).

Gilbert, N. (ed.) (1993), *Researching Social Life* (London: Sage).

Green, E. and Singleton, C, (2006), 'Risk Bodies at Leisure: Young Women Negotiating Space and Place', *Sociology* 40:5, 853–71.

Hall, S. (1990), 'Cultural identity and Diaspora', in Rutherford, J. (ed.) (1990), *Identity: Community, Culture, Difference* (London: Lawrence and Wishart).

Hall, S. (1992), 'The Question of Cultural Identity' in Hall, S. et al. (eds) (1992), *Modernity and its Futures* (Cambridge: Polity Press).

Hollway, W. (1984), 'Gender difference and the production of subjectivity', in Henriques, J. et al. (eds) (1984), *Changing the Subject: Psychology, Social Regulation and Subjectivity* (London: Methuen).

Hollway, W. and Jefferson, T. (2000), *Doing Qualitative Research Differently: Free Association, Narrative and the Interview Method* (London: Sage).

Hough, M. et al. (2005), *Trends in Violent Crime Since 1999/2000* (London: The Institute for Criminal Policy Research, School of Law, Kings College).

Margo, J. et al. (2006), *Freedom's Orphans* (London: Institute for Public Policy Research).

Messerschmidt, J. W. (1994), 'Schooling, Masculinities and Youth Crime by White Boys', in Newburn, T. and Stanko, E. A. (eds) (1994), *Just Boys Doing Business?* (London: Routledge).

Office for National Statistics (2005) *Living in Britain 2005* (published online May 2005), <http://www.statistics.gov.uk>

Petersen, A. (2003), 'Research on Men and Masculinities: Some Implications of Recent Theory for Future Work', *Men and Masculinities* 6:1, 54–69.

Rutherford, J. (ed.) (1990), *Identity: Community, Culture, Difference* (London: Lawrence and Wishart).

Stoudt, B. G. (2006), 'You're Either In or Out: School Violence and Discipline And The Reproduction of Hegemonic Masculinity', *Men and Masculinities* 1:18, 273–87.

Tulloch, J. and Lupton, D. (2003) *Risk and Everyday Life* (London: Sage).

Wetherell, M. (1998), 'Positioning and interpretative repertoires: conversation analysis and post-structuralism in dialogue', *Discourse and Society* 9:3, 387–416.

Wetherell, M. and Edley, N. (1999), 'Negotiating Hegemonic Masculinity: Imaginary Positions and Psycho-Discursive Practices', *Feminism and Psychology* 9:335–56.

Whitehead, S. M. (2002), *Men and Masculinities* (Cambridge: Polity).

Woolfit, R. (1993), 'Analysing accounts', in Gilbert, N. (ed.).

Chapter 6

Violence, Risk and Identity: 'Doing Gender' or Negotiation of Structural Barriers to Non-violent Alternatives?

Wendy Laverick

Introduction

We know very little about how people define risk (Tulloch and Lupton 2003, 16). Yet, interest in risk factors contributing to violence continues to be high as professionals search for tools to identify those 'at-risk' and seek empirically based intervention strategies that might reduce violent behaviour (Pettit 2004, 194). Risk assessment is however, an inexact science and the methods used still contain serious shortcomings (Doyle and Dolan 2002; Stone 2002). That is despite any limitations regarding the predictive accuracy of risk assessment models and the lack of guaranteed outcomes (Sheldrick, 1999), 'considerable support can be found for theoretical models positing that life experiences ... cumulate to increase the risk of antisocial and violent behaviour (Pettit 2004, 194).

There is, however, a difficulty which arises within this literature. Namely the question identified by Margolin and Gordis (2004) as to why some who experience risk factors show negative outcomes and others appear to be more resilient. They conclude that 'explanatory models of individual and contextual factors that either buffer against or exacerbate the effects of violence are needed' (Margolin and Gordis 2004, 154). This view is shared by Sheldrick (1999) and Pettit (2004) who critique traditional models of risk assessment for failing to examine resilience in the presence of adversity when examining crime and violence. As such, a more complex and dynamic model of the individual and risk is advocated.

This charge regarding a general failure to examine individual processes of resilience has emerged within recent critiques of risk theory including the work of Beck (1992), Giddens (1994), Tulloch and Lupton (2003) and Dean, (1997). These macro approaches are challenged on the basis that risks are conceived as external influences upon individuals allowing little room for agency. Tulloch and Lupton (2003) promote a poststructuralist analysis as the best means to approach the lived experiences and agency of individuals. Accordingly, the present study detailed in this chapter employs a more micro or everyday approach to risk.

Following Tulloch and Lupton (2003), this chapter seeks to examine what kind of risks men and women with established histories of violence take or avoid and why. It will explore how individuals construct identity in and through various discourses in the course of their everyday lives. It will be suggested that risks are intertwined with social actors' identity formation and social relations. Risks associated with violence are consequently viewed as discourses, which are constructed and reconstructed by social actors within particular social contexts. Significantly, it is suggested that risks can only be made sense of by taking account of contextual and biographical data. The present study, influenced by Foucault (1998), attempts to shed light upon the way that discourses are utilised and provide meanings, which influence and organise actions and self-concepts. The motivation for 'resistances' or choices amongst different discourses (Foucault 2002) are what interests this book and therefore remains the implicit focus for the present chapter.

The Study

The aim of this chapter is to contextualise a number of risk factors associated with individual propensity towards violence within the narrative accounts of male and female offenders with established histories of violence. Each account sheds light upon individual processes of identity construction, risk taking, risk avoidance and the interplay between dominant discourses of gender, class and generation.

Men, it seems, are disproportionately represented within official statistics, self-report studies and victimisation surveys alike. Thus men commit ninety percent of violent crime (Campbell and Muncer 1994, 332). As a result it has been suggested that the most prominent 'fact' about crime is the sex of the offender (see Newburn and Stanko 1994; Gelsthorpe, 2002). The 'masculinity turn' embodies a growing literature which places great analytic value upon examining men as gendered subjects when considering crime (Smith and McVie 2003). Sex and class enter as significant risk factors, thus Messerschmidt (1993) developed the notion of criminality, including violence, as 'resources' for the accomplishment of gender. Crime therefore became integrally linked up with an individual's masculine gender identity.

This position is not without challenge. In parallel fashion to the risk theory previously discussed, macro studies of masculinity (Messerschmidt 1993; 1994; Polk 1994) failed to account for agency and resistance. Furthermore, an additional issue has emerged, for it is now recognised that women are not without the capacity for aggression (Campbell and Muncer 1994; Smith and McVie 2003). Consequently, the difficulty with employing a gendered orientation which conflates violence with masculinity is that violence perpetrated by women becomes problematic.

By way of departure, Miller (2002a; 2002b) argues that individuals have the capacity to draw from a variety of schemas (including incompatible or contradictory ones) when engaging in social action. Miller's Foucauldian position conceives the self as subject to reconstruction dependent upon social contexts created by different discourses. Within this position, the individual's relationship to risk relies on the construction of self and how one relates to such discourse. Accordingly, the adoption of particular schemas within specific contexts is a process that warrants further investigation. The present study enables the participants themselves to describe their motivation for action rather than presuming that actions are always undertaken in accordance to the accomplishment of normative gender. This research is therefore intended to develop upon previous research into the area of violence exploring behaviour and the 'choices' made by offenders as to whether to utilise violence and how they negotiate the risks implicit in these choices.

To this end a total of thirty semi-structured interviews were carried out within two prisons in the North of England. The criterion for inclusion was an individual's established history of violence. Interviewees comprised an equal number of men and women and a range of ages, criminal records, educational attainment and occupations.

Contextual Risk Factors: Criminal Areas

The interview data highlight issues which have been identified as personal, social or contextual 'risk factors' for violence within the psychological literature (Langstrom and Grann 2002; Youngstrom et al. 2003; Tiffin and Kaplan 2004). It was clear from the interviews that the risks to which these individuals were exposed were frequently attributed to growing up within violent neighbourhoods and/or families (contextual risk factor/personal risk factor), and that violence was often considered 'normal':

> Anne: I were brought up in a mining area, it's a bit rough and people fought. Men fought on a Saturday night in front of the pub. Women fought over kids arguing and it were that generation from a working class background. Fighting were normal.

> David: The area I was brought up in, violence was a main factor. That's how you got your respect, everybody understood it, that's how everybody acted. From knocking about with older people, I've listened to conversations and I was learning. It obviously stayed with me so that I knew how to act in situations when the time did come. It was like that was my learning ground really, my neighbourhood in which I grew up.

Geographical location, generation and class featured strongly within many of the accounts supporting Tulloch and Lupton's (2003, 25) finding that the risks to which people feel they are exposed are phrased through their own structural position.

While there is much evidence within criminological literature to suggest that risk factors are associated with aggression; the social reproduction of criminal attitudes within 'criminal areas' has long been recognised (Vold et al. 1998). Social disorganisation theorists (see Shaw and McKay, 1972) assume there is a normative consensus against delinquency within society at large. The cultural transmission of norms also features strongly within the literature on risk. Thus, Tulloch and Lupton

(2003), suggest aspects of risk-consciousness appear to be shared across cultural groups. Their work advocates investigation into cultural attitudes and contexts when evaluating interpretations and responses to risk (Tulloch and Lupton, 2003, 1). In the following section, normative systems will be examined. It will be revealed that the interviewees often reported being confronted with a variety of discourses surrounding the use and non-use of violence as a means of conflict resolution. Initially, norms challenging the use of violence will be presented, followed by pro-violence proscriptions conceptualised as self-defence, both as recommendation and coercion.

Norms Discouraging Violence

Anne and Alan's interviews illustrate parental discouragement regarding male-on-female violence on the basis of age and gender disparity:

> Interviewer: What did your mum say to you when she broke up your fight?
>
> Anne: She told me brother off for hitting me cos I were youngest and I were a girl.
>
> Alan: I haven't had any fights with either of my sisters, I don't hit girls. My parents wouldn't have allowed it. My parents were quite strict with that. I don't believe in hitting women.
>
> Interviewer: Do you have a reason?
>
> Alan: If you hit a woman you are not a man.

Alan's account challenges Messerschmidt's (1993) view that violence is a means of gender identity construction; instead Alan perceived violence against female recipients as potentially undermining one's gender identity. Social action is therefore mediated by normative beliefs regarding gender, the appropriateness of particular forms of action and the particular participants involved. Surprisingly, many of the female interviewees also appeared to have internalised this prohibition against hitting women:

> Eve: I'd rather fight with a bloke than with a bird. At the end of the day I fight with my fists and I wouldn't think twice over picking a bottle up and smashing it, sticking it in their face. I will fight a girl but I'll punch her.

The transmission of norms discouraging violence was revealed to be extremely complex and subject to contingencies. Brenda's account presents contradictory discourses expressed by family members:

> Brenda: To me violence is a coward's way of getting out of things. It's what my dad always taught me. But then me brothers turned round and said 'no, fighting is the best way

of getting out of everything' so I had two opinions contradicting each other. I used to do the middle thing, I used to fight if I couldn't get out of it but if I could then I would.

Evidently, Brenda's brothers did not conceive Brenda's gender as a barrier to violence either as perpetrator or recipient.

> Brenda: I got taught that you fight lads not lasses. A lot of the lads that I used to fight with used to go 'I'm not hitting her she's a girl', until I hit them and then they were like 'are you sure you're a girl?' And my brothers would say 'she's been brought up exactly the same as us and she can fight exactly the same as us if push comes to shove'.

This contrasts with the attitude expressed by her eldest brother:

> Brenda: He was the only one who used to try to guide. If I got into a fight he used to be like 'you didn't have to fight then', and I'd be 'yeah I did'. Whereas my other brothers would go 'go on'. [My eldest brother] was the only one who used to go 'but you're a girl. You fight girls'.

It was not fighting *per se* which Brenda's older brother discouraged, rather fighting between the sexes. Interestingly, the notice taken by the interviewees between contradictory discourses was contingent upon existing relationships, and for some of the male interviewees, the sex of the individual giving the advice. Hence, David dismissed his mother's advice 'to walk away' from potential confrontations, explaining that 'women say things like that'.

Evidently, (and in support of Tulloch and Lupton 2003, 1) understandings about the ways in which risk is dealt with and experienced are conceived by several of the respondents in terms of their memberships of cultures as well as through personal experience. In contrast to the existence of a normative anti-violence consensus, an alternative position is raised regarding the possibility that large sections of society do not necessarily disapprove of violent behaviour (Vold et al. 1998). This theme has been conceptualised as comprising 'definitions favourable to violation of law' (Matza and Sykes 1961). It refers to areas where delinquent attitudes, rationalisations and motives are prevalent. These normative systems are believed to exist in opposition to, or in competition with, the middle class value system, or in relation to the encouragement, support or pressure to act delinquently by significant others. The existence of parental deviance and pro-criminal attitudes are the focus of the following section.

Violence as 'Self-Defence'

The previous section demonstrated the existence of a normative code based upon gender and age which mediates the use of violence as appropriate and/or desirable action when faced with particular situations. Interestingly Anne's mother did not employ the same instruction for female-upon-female aggression:

> Anne: Me mum certainly encouraged me to stick up for meself and to stand me ground …
> [A] girl scratched me in a fight at school and me mum got really angry that she'd marked
> me face and she said 'who's gunna hurt hardest, me or her? You will go back out there and
> you will hit her back'.

Anne describes being encouraged to utilise violence as a reaction to physical
victimisation. This contrasts sharply with the guidance distributed to her brother.
These incidents reveal contingencies in the conduct norm prescriptions of Anne's
mother which are mediated by 'age', 'gender', the relationship between the victim
and perpetrator and the discourse of 'self-defence'.

The discourse of self-defence also emerges within Helen's account:

> Helen: If I were arguing with anyone, me dad would say 'smack her' [laughs]. Well that
> would be everybody's recommendation, all me aunties and that, 'give her a whack'. I
> think that they thought it was good that I was sticking up for myself, cos some people are
> weak aren't they. You shouldn't let anyone bully you.

This notion of self-defence appears to be linked to Sykes and Matza (1957) 'techniques
of neutralisation' which have been described as freeing the individual from social
control. Many of the respondents considered that their actions constituted rightful
retaliation for the unjust behaviour of others. Consequently there was a 'denial
of the victim' within several of the accounts. Above, Anne and Helen's accounts
demonstrate that family members shared similar attitudes regarding self-defence,
encouraging retaliation following incidents of (same-sex) bullying.

The following accounts of Eve, Henry and David express coercion in the
transmission of normative expectations to utilise violence.

> Eve: We used to come in crying from a fight and my dad used to make us go out there and
> fight with them again, watch us and if we got beaten again he used to beat us in front of
> them and say 'right, fight them again'. Me dad was basically a bastard. He sent me brother
> out with a hammer for the kids next door.

Henry attempted to prevent another child from being bullied by two boys. He was
subsequently 'beaten up' and returned home:

> Henry: I was gutted 'cos I got beat up, but I knew who they were so I went back with a
> stick.
>
> Interviewer: For what reason?
>
> Henry: 'Cos I went home and then me dad saw that I'd been beat up so he told me that if
> you don't go back and sort it out I'll sort you out, so I didn't have a choice really,
>
> Interviewer: Were you concerned about your dad?

Henry: Oh god yeah, he's about seven foot two, he's a big Arab. Afterwards, he was like nice one, cos he dropped me off in the car and watched me and then I got back in the car and he took me home.

These accounts demonstrate that often a 'failure' to defend oneself is negatively viewed by some parents who recommend, encourage, or coerce their children into violent retaliation. These norms were transmitted by mothers and fathers to male and female children. These respondents did not feel that they had a choice. These attitudes were frequently passed on from generation to generation as David's account demonstrates.

David recalled an incident in which he had been victimised. He described his father's response upon his return home;

David: He's gone, get out there and give him a lamping, or I'll give you one. So I've gone 'he's bigger than me', and he's gone, if you can't use your hands pick something up, so I've picked an iron bar up and I welded him with it [laughs], and then after that, you find, violence don't come your way very often with people who know ya. You get that respect.

David's example is important in that it provides insight into the transmission of pro-violent attitudes between siblings. David's brother is described as 'quiet', and 'introverted'. One day, David witnessed his brother being bullied:

David: I've gone off me head and I've threatened to punch me brother's face in if he didn't act. I forced him into violence, so he dealt with the chap and after he gained the respect in the school but it was something he didn't want to do. After then he was never troubled, I suppose, in a way he learnt to hold his own.

Interviewer: What would have happened if you hadn't taught your brother to stand up for himself?

David: He would have been the victim, he'd of been the victim of bullying.

These accounts illustrate how discourses about violence are utilised and transmitted as a means of risk aversion embedded within particularised biographies situated within family and neighbourhood contexts.

In the following section, personal and social risk factors will be examined in order to shed light upon motivation for violent action and the risks implicit within these decisions. In support of Tulloch and Lupton (2003, 11) It will become evident that many of the respondents employ rational discourses to account for their use (and avoidance) of violence in addition to non-violent alternatives.

From Victim to Perpetrator

Eve's interview depicts direct victimisation (personal risk factors) in the form of physical and sexual abuse. Aggression between her parents was described as routine and Eve explained that she had witnessed violence as part of her everyday life. These experiences were attributed as significant in locating the aetiology of her violent behaviour: Eve stated, 'If I had a different upbringing I wouldn't be here [in prison] today'

Gender is significant and recognised as an important issue mediating the everyday risks faced by Eve throughout her early life:

> Eve: I was like Cinderella. I had to play mum to me brothers at the age of eleven. I had to cook them a proper dinner, do me dad's washing, ironing, and then he [Eve's father] got me pregnant and I had to have a termination.

Following her mother's departure from the home Eve was forced to step into her mother's domestic and sexual role.

> Eve: Me dad pulled clothes out from the draws and I had to do all the washing by the time he got back from the pub. He'd also write dates in dust, or put a mark on the door frame so that he knew it ain't been dusted. He'd done it to me mam as well. He beat me so bad with a belt that day. He slung me and [my brother] on the bed and made him have sex with me. I was screaming, fighting with him and then me dad has slapped me on the bottom of me legs with a belt so I had to let him do it. One of my brothers beats up his wife, another writes dates, for his girlfriend.

Eve's sex and the gender norms and expectations of her father clearly influenced the forms of victimisation she became subject to within her family. As a consequence, Eve conceived it normal for women to be physically assaulted without repercussion;

> Interviewer: Do people expect you to behave in a particular way?
>
> Eve: Yeah, I suppose so. In the children's home, saying 'we'll make a lady of you yet', but they never did. 'You shouldn't swear', 'shouldn't go about hitting people', 'pleases and thank you'. It's like, a bloke is supposed to hit a woman and we're not supposed to do anything back. But no-one is hitting me. I will hit them back at the end of the day.

Tulloch and Lupton (2003) argue that risk may serve as a means of conforming to, or challenging gender stereotypes. The latter is evident within Eve's narrative. Eve explained that she fought with male authority figures including care workers, police officers and custody staff.

> Eve: I can't trust men me. I get very hot headed and I will fight a man me. Like if you're in a club dancing and some man touches you, me head flips. All I'll see when I'm hitting them is my dad, cos at that age I couldn't do nothing to defend myself.

When Eve's partner became domestically violent towards her, Eve's solution was extreme:

> Eve: He was drinking and he's give me such a punch and as I've gone flying off the bed me baby's come with me. I had a big lump, split me eye. One punch I got from him so I boiled up the chip fat. I couldn't do it so I got the hammer out of the toolbox and I hit him three times with the hammer while he was asleep.
>
> Interviewer: What were you thinking?
>
> Eve: I was just fed up of being a fucking punchbag. As the years went on it was me hitting him.

Violence comprised a real risk within Eve's encounters with men. Yet, the function of violence ultimately altered with violence eventually becoming a risk aversive behaviour in the form of pre-emptive action. Below, Eve and Irene's accounts illustrate how recipients became perpetrators within a cycle of violence:

> Eve: I did have one nice boyfriend. I didn't have sex with him, he gave me anything but he ended up being my punchbag. I knew that he'd never hit me back and I just took the piss.
>
> Irene: [My husband] was an alcoholic, he would come in and it was 'dinner is not on the table' and he'd knock me around, smash up the house, smash me up. I ended his life for him. He fractured my skull and the kids got taken into care. I had enough, I just wanted to get away and when he came after me, that's when I ended his life. When you've been through that, and that person is in your face shouting at you, and all the flashbacks. It is not coming back from just yesterday, its coming back from when you first met him, it's like a time clock.

Although the form of victimisation differed between interviewees (including sexual abuse, domestic violence, and physical abuse) it became clear that the participants consciously calculated the risks of employing violence over the risks of being subject to victimisation. It is interesting that these sentiments were also paralleled by a number of the accounts depicting bullying. These various manifestations of victimisation were viewed as significant in instigating violence as a method of self-defence, pre-emptive action or revenge for past injustices. However, the recipient of violence need not necessarily have been the original perpetrator. Indeed, as the discussions of alternative strategies will reveal, experiences of victimisation are strongly associated with physical assaults upon entirely innocent persons, or self-harm to the individuals themselves. Helen and Alan describe this process:

> Helen: It scared me because I thought, if I've let someone do something to me then I could let someone batter me again. I would never let it happen again, the same with boys. I've never been hit off a boyfriend ever. I think because me dad used to hit me mam and that

and I swore that you know, no man would ever hit me. That is probably why I've turned it round, cos I've been scared of them doing it to me. I think it is just insecurity.

Alan: From school I wasn't going to allow myself to be bullied or ripped off or picked on. I couldn't allow it to happen again. I won't back down to anybody. It's like a macho image sort of thing, to show the other person that I'm not scared of them.

In this section it is clear that 'risk knowledges' are based upon normative discourses transmitted within and outside of the family, through observation of everyday phenomena in addition to the behaviour of others around them. This lends support to Berger and Luckman's (1967) contention that as a result of the socialisation process, the individual cannot stand outside discourse since social reality is both normative and explanatory. Failure to employ violence as self-defence or as a mean of avoiding potential victimisation held real consequences, from disapproval and/or punishment from family members, to actual victimisation. Importantly, such consequences were not viewed as static and many of the respondents reflected upon the changing functions (risk embracing and risk aversive) and consequences (both positive and negative) of utilising violence.

Anne: It wasn't until you grew up that you saw the dangers and implications of actually physically fighting someone. I just took it as ordinary. When I were twenty-four I were fighting with me sister. She bullied me. She used to physically push me around and this day I'd just lost the plot and I gave her a good hiding. She called the police … My parents never forgave her for involving the police and that I got a conviction. I still don't speak to her to this day. For years I took the hidings from her. I never called the police. I'm not saying that it's right what I did but I am saying it should have been resolved within the family.

Here, violence is conceived as both a risk aversive and risk embracing behaviour. Anne, on the basis of previous experience of victimisation attempted to avoid the risk of further victimisation through the utilisation of physical violence. For Anne, the risk of experiencing public embarrassment was enough to trigger a violent response although this is contextualised within a lifetime of such incidents:

Anne: She did it to me before. She'd do it in front of my friends, she'd do it in front of her husband, she'd do it anywhere and I think because it was in the middle of the day and people were getting on and off the bus I just thought I'm not having this. I don't like it.

Violence is subsequently conceived as a risk embracing behaviour:

Anne: Hindsight is a wonderful thing. There is a different way round but I didn't know. I hadn't got the tools of growing up when I were young. There are always consequences to your action, hence the fight with my sister. She ended up in hospital and I ended up in court. She ended up with my parents not speaking to her and they didn't speak to her until they died. I shoulder some of the responsibility for that.

Compare Anne's account with that of Elliott:

> Elliott: I didn't think he could bully me anymore so I used to tell this to all the people, you know bragging about it. Anyway, someone went and told him and the next thing I knew, we were in the cloakroom and he just set about me. I got the better of him this time. Afterwards, even though I'd won I still felt a little unsure of myself with him. He'd been able to get the better of me all these years and I still felt, even though I'd had that little victory, then come another day he might be able to do it again. As I got older the tables reversed. I started bullying him.

Despite increasing confidence arising as a result of enhanced physical development during puberty, Elliott's original feelings of anxiety were not eradicated;

> Elliott: Everyone had high expectations if I got into a fight of me winning. But I think, deep down I've always known that that is not the case. I've always got that little boy inside of me that used to get bullied. One afternoon I attacked a lad and he turned round and got the better, it were in front of my friends and my girlfriend and I were made to look like a bit of an idiot. I remember going home that day feeling a bit bad. Since then, I've never really been one hundred per cent confident in myself. I think that a lot of my self confidence came from the buzz of people seeing me in a certain way, Elliott the headcase, Elliott the hardman. But when you know it is not true it puts a lot of pressure on you. I'm scared of losing my reputation, losing my popularity. I always used to look up to certain people who were known to be hard men. That's how it started off. I no longer look up to people for being hard, I see things differently now.

Non-violent Strategies

In the previous section, Anne and Elliott's accounts illustrate how negative consequences of utilising physical violence transformed into protective factors against employing future violence. In this section, Eve's account sheds light upon desistance from violence and the decision making processes involved in employing non-violent alternatives.

Eve explained that she employed various strategies at different points throughout her life. Eve attempted suicide on numerous occasions in an effort to stop her father from abusing her ('I wanted to be dead so he couldn't touch me no more'). Eve also used drugs and alcohol explaining that 'it blocked everything out, the nightmares stopped and I stopped wetting myself'. Self-harm was another method employed to manage her emotional situation:

> Eve: When people get on my nerves and I feel like I am going to explode I cut myself and it releases pressure from me. I bottle a lot of things up and then explode. I used to cut myself so that I didn't get in trouble and get nicked for ABH or GBH. It calms me down, but at the end of the day it is no good because of the scars. I'll take it out on myself, it's either that or I'll kick the shit out of someone and it is not their fault.

Eve described a particular incident in which she confided in a friend thereby using verbal communication as an alternative to physical violence or self-harm. This potentially risk aversive behaviour (in the sense that violence might have been avoided), ultimately proved to be a risky enterprise in itself:

> Eve: I told [my friend] about the baby but one day we had an argument. She said 'at least I didn't get pregnant by me dad'. I really battered her. I bit through her face and everything. I nearly killed her. That killed me inside. That tore me apart that did.
>
> Interviewer: What effect did that have on you?
>
> Eve: I wouldn't let nobody in. I'm now one of these people, 'I'm a soldier, I'm alright'. I am there for somebody else but I won't tell them my problems.

The risks implicit within verbal communication are reiterated within Alan's account:

> Alan: If something is bothering me I don't talk to my parents or to anybody else. I just let it all build up inside me and unfortunately it's my parents who get the full brunt of it.. I don't feel comfortable talking to somebody one to one if I have a problem. I find it hard trusting people. I've shown my emotions before and people have just taken the piss out of me. If I do show my emotion I do it in private so no-one can see me.

Eve and Alan's accounts shed light upon the choices made as to whether to utilise violence or non-violent alternatives (verbal communication, self-harm, alcohol and drug abuse) as coping strategies to deal with emotional life events and the negotiation of risks implicit in these choices. It is evident that non-violent options were frequently conceptualised in terms of the risks of being viewed as 'weak' or as opening up the individual for potential victimisation. These decisions were rooted within each of the respondents' subjective experiences and the consequences of their actions. These accounts contrast with several of the male accounts who employ a gendered discourse in their rationalisations.

David alluded to gender, class and generation to account for his father's attitude to non-violent emotional expression;

> David: Me old man, his environment, where he grew up, men were men, they don't say these things, you keep what you've got in there locked in. I suppose I learnt as well to be like that. We've never sat down and had a conversation. We talk around things. I would have liked him to understand me and worked with me.

When asked what he thought caused his violence, David explained:

> David: My temper comes from like my emotions. They probably could be used as a weapon you know. These are the tools that I need. I think understanding of how to deal with that emotion and how to channel it.

Henry also highlighted the connection between managing emotion and violence:

> Henry: Being emotional, talking about your emotions or crying just wasn't done. You just don't talk about stuff like that. I mean my sister's may have talked to my mum about stuff like that but like my father was a Muslim, and as a Muslim you don't talk about your emotions, you deal with them, that's it, it's what you're taught, if you've got a problem you deal with it, if you get angry you deal with it, that's the way it is.

Conclusion: Violence and Identity Construction

Criminologists have begun to reassess gender issues and assumptions, and a number are now beginning to explore the possible links between criminal behaviour and masculine affirmation. For many, a man's masculine identity does play a role in his involvement in criminal behaviour (Daly and Wilson 1988; Polk 1994; Messerschmidt 1993; 1994; 1999; Newburn and Stanko 1994; Mac an Ghaill 1996). However, the exact influence and salience attributed to masculine gender identity has become a site of contention. Exactly what sort of role 'masculinity' occupies in relation to crime and specifically violent crime remains unanswered. With a renewed interest in female offenders the links between gender identity and crime is only now starting to be asked in terms of femininity (Laidler and Hunt 2001; Miller 2002a; 2002b; Kirkwood 2003). This chapter has shed light upon decisions to utilise violence or non-violent alternatives and how individuals negotiate the risks implicit within these choices.

This text, 'Risks, Identities and the Everyday'; explores how individuals must negotiate a social world where identities, statuses and norms are either fixed or fluid depending on context. Each social context is considered to be controlled and demarcated by discourses to be interpreted, challenged, negotiated or accepted. This chapter has provided support for viewing individuals as embedded within structures of gender, class, age and generation, illustrating how such structures shape responses to risk. In support of Tulloch and Lupton (2003:11), the data present risks as positive choices for some individuals. This study also lends support to the view that 'lay knowledge' of risk is highly localised reflecting membership of social and cultural networks which influence the negotiation and interpretation of risk.

Specifically, in support of Miller (2002a), the interview data challenges the assumption that action (and in this case violent action) is always taken with a goal of accomplishing normative gender identity. Several interviewees commented that they had to negotiate a variety of discourses regarding violence, including a normative prohibition against the use of violence towards women and a normative expectation to utilise violence as a means of self-defence. Gender, class, generation and age were seen to intersect and mediate social action supporting Miller's (2002a) observation that individuals have the capacity to draw on a variety of competing or contradictory schemas and facets of identity when selecting between various subject positions and modes of action. The interview data illustrates how risk discourses are therefore made sense of and also contribute to self-identity (as victims, as able to defend one-self or as perpetrator).

It became evident that violence comprised a real risk within the everyday lives of the respondents as personal, social and contextual risks. Light is therefore shed upon the way in which discourses of risk emerge or are constructed through observation, direct experience or normative codes to which each individual is subject. Early desistance from violence, eventual use of violence and in some cases, utilisation of non-violent alternatives were, frequently associated with both positive and negative consequences which were seen to alter throughout the life-course. Risk discourses are therefore not static but complex and dynamic utilised by social actors who employ reflexivity as a heuristic device to provide meaning and guide action.

Gender, while not the only salient facet of identity influencing social action, does retain explanatory value within some (although by no means all) of the narrative accounts. However the position is far more complex than originally conceived. Violence, as a form of risk aversive (or risk embracing behaviour) can be viewed as both a vehicle for identity construction and a reaction to it in addition to fulfilling numerous other non-gender specific functions. Many of the female interviewees employed gendered discourses when discussing structural inequalities and the associated risks faced by women in society and by themselves within the context of their own families. Gender also entered into several female accounts when considering particular risks faced within everyday encounters with men. A particularly interesting observation when comparing the male and female accounts is how violence was frequently conceived as a means of challenging gender stereotypes or inequalities within several of the female interviews. This reiterates the significance of appreciating resistance and agency in addition to conformity with normative expectations of gender when discussing violence (see Foucault 1998). Within those male accounts, which comprised references to gendered discourse, violence, self-defence and masculinity, were often conflated alluding to an association between power and 'adult' maleness. This of course contrasted sharply against their subjective experiences of victimisation as male children and thus age and physical status were frequently an overlapping theme within these accounts.

This suggests that the individual's relationship to risk depends on the construction of self and how one relates to different discourses mediated by age, body, and class in addition to other conceptual schema. It is important to note that discourses of violence intersected with discourses of masculinity within a few of the male accounts while the female accounts tended to rely upon other schema to explain similar phenomena. This indicates that the male respondents may have had access to a form of discourse to which the female respondents (by virtue of their sex) were structurally blocked from utilising. Finally, gender also featured within a number of the male interviews as a barrier from other modes of non-violent action and/or resources. Although again, gender was not the only facet of identity to be implicated within this structural exclusion as generation, class, age and religion were also seen as intersecting.

Ultimately, a number of recurring themes and discourses across the entire interviewee group were identified including the transmission of norms and expectations regarding violence, subjective experiences of victimisation and barriers to the utilisation of non-violent alternatives. While it is essential to contextualise the accounts within their individual biographies it is interesting that gender discourses were only relied upon by a small proportion of the respondents to account for their access to and exclusion from modes of social action.

References

Beck, U. (1992), *Risk Society: Towards A New Modernity* (London: Sage).

Berger, P. and Luckmann, T. (1967), *The Social Construction of Reality* (London: Anchor Books).

Campbell, A. and Muncer, S. (1994), 'Men and the Meaning of Violence', Archer, J. (ed.) (1994), *Male Violence* (London: Routledge).

Daly, M. and Wilson, M. (1988), *Homicide* (New York: Aldine De Gruyter).

Dean, M. (1997), 'Sociology after society', in Owen, D. (ed.) (1997), *Sociology after Postmodernism* (London: Sage).

Doyle, M. and Dolan, M. (2002), 'Violence Risk Assessment: Combining Actuarial and Clinical Information to Structure Clinical Judgements for the Formulation and Management of Risk', *Journal of Psychiatric and Mental Health Nursing* 9:649–57.

Foucault, M. (1998) *History of Sexuality: Will to Knowledge* (London: Penguin Books).

—— (2002), *Power: Essential Works of Foucault 1954–1984* (London: Penguin Books).

Gelsthorpe, L. (2002), 'Feminism and Criminology', in Maguire, M. (2002) *The Oxford Handbook of Criminology* (Oxford: Oxford University Press).

Giddens, A. (1994), 'Living in a Post-Traditional Society' in Beck, U. et al. (1994) *Reflexive Modernization: Politics, Tradition and Aesthetics in the Modern Social Order* (Cambridge: Polity Press).

Kirkwood, D. (2003), 'Female Perpetrated Homicide in Victoria Between 1985 and 1995', *The Australian and New Zealand Journal of Criminology* 36:2, 152–72.

Laidler, K. and Hunt, G. (2001), 'Accomplishing Femininity Among the Girls in the Gang', *British Journal of Criminology* 41:656–78.

Langstrom, N. and Grann, M. (2002), 'Psychopathy and Violent Recidivism Among Young Criminal Offenders', *Acta Psychiatrica Scandinavica* 106:412, 86–92.

Mac an Ghaill, M. (ed.) (1996), *Understanding Masculinities* (Buckingham: Open University Press).

Margolin, G. and Gordis, E. (2004), 'Children's Exposure to Violence in the Family and Community: Current Directions in Psychological Science', *American Psychological Society* 13:4, 152–55.

Matza, D. and Sykes, G. (1961), 'Juvenile Delinquency and Subterranean Values', *American Sociological Review*, 26:712–19.

Messerschmidt, J. (1993), 'Varieties of "Real Men"', in O'Toole, L. et al. (eds.) (1997), *Gender Violence: Interdisciplinary Perspectives* (London: New York University Press).

—— (1994), 'Schooling, Masculinities, and Youth Crime by White Boys', in Newburn, T. and Stanko, E. (eds.) (1994), *Just Boys Doing Business* (London: Routledge).

—— (1999), 'Making Bodies Matter: Adolescent Masculinities, the Body, and Varieties of Violence', *Theoretical Criminology* 3:2, 197–220.

Miller, J. (2002a), 'The Strengths and Limits of "Doing Gender" for Understanding Street Crime', *Theoretical Criminology* 6:4, 433–60.

Miller, J. (2002b), 'Reply to Messerschmidt', *Theoretical Criminology* 6:4, 477–80.

Newburn, T. and Stanko, E. (eds). (1994), *Just Boys Doing Business* (London: Routledge).

Pettit, G. (2004), 'Violent Children in Developmental Perspective: Risk and Protective Factors and the Mechanisms Through Which They (May) Operate': Current Directions in Psychological Science', *American Psychological Society* 13:5, 194–97.

Polk, K. (1994), *When Men Kill: Scenarios of Masculine Violence* (Hong Kong: Cambridge University Press).

Shaw, C. R. and McKay, H. D. (1972), *Juvenile Delinquency and Urban Areas* (London: Phoenix Books).

Sheldrick, C. (1999), 'Practitioner Review: The Assessment and Management of Risk in Adolescents', *Journal of Child Psychology* 40:4, 507–18.

Smith, D. and McVie, S. (2003), 'Theory and Method in the Edinburgh Study of Youth Transitions and Crime', *British Journal of Criminology* 43:169–95.

Stone, M. (2002), 'Prediction of Violent Recidivism', *Acta Psychiatrica Scandinavica* 106:412, 44–6.

Sykes, G. and Matza, D. (1957), 'Techniques of Neutralization: A Theory of Delinquency', *American Sociological Review* 22:6, 664–70.

Tiffin, P. and Kaplan, C. (2004), 'Dangerous Children: Assessment and Management of Risk', *Child and Adolescent Mental Health* 9:2, 56–64.

Tulloch, J. and Lupton, D. (2003), *Risk and Everyday Life* (London: Sage).

Vold, G. B. et al. (1998), *Theoretical Criminology* (Oxford: Oxford University Press).

Youngstrom, E. et al. (2003), 'Exploring Violence Exposure, Stress, Protective Factors and Behavioural Problems Among Inner-City Youth', *American Journal of Community Psychology* 32:1/2, 115–29.

Chapter 7

'Get with the Programme': Human Resource Management a Risky Strategy?

Sal Watt

Introduction

> oh we have got this brilliant new thing and we are going to do this and you know full well that either there will be a change of government or a new policy or something else will come in and it will never get there (Shelley).

Phrases such as 'risk management' and 'risk assessment' abound in the business world and workplace. Indeed more recently, they can be heard appropriated within everyday discourse. In origin these phrases stem from an organisational discourse or 'managerial speak' that is usually linked to some form of organisational change (Legge 1995; Collins 1998; Senior 2002); more specifically changes that impact on the everyday lives of workers and, as such, constitutes and is understood and experienced in terms of risk (Collins 1998; Dickens 1998; Beck 2000; Ezzy 2001). This chapter will consider risk and HRM (Human Resource Management) when used as a strategy for change from several perspectives. First it will briefly consider the nefarious use of the word 'risk' in the workplace as a catch-all for visible, practical and accountable risk. It will then consider the utilisation of HRM as a macro strategy to effect organisational and cultural change. The discursive effects of HRM as a strategy will then be juxtaposed with the everyday experiences of civil servants as they negotiate its discourses at a micro level as part of their everyday working lives. In conclusion the chapter will consider the effects of HRM at a meso leve – that is at the point where the discursive meaning of HRM as an organisationally imposed change strategy interacts or is interpreted by civil servants.

Framing Risk in the Workplace

Assessing risk in the workplace can encompass any type of financial or physical loss, disruption, injury or, post the attacks of '9/11', terrorist destruction. Typically it is framed within a 'Health and Safety' discourse and in very broad terms 'risk management' can be defined as the pre-empting and avoidance of risk while 'risk assessment' is the tool or practical means by which to quantify and counter potential risks (Coulsen-Thomas 1997; Reason 1997; Lupton 1999; Edwards and Bowen 2002;

Fone and Young 2005). At a practical level, risk assessment, in terms of Human Resource recruitment functions more typically in personality typing, risk propensity and decision making and personnel welfare issues such as stress (Kahneman and Tversky 1984; DeCenzo and Silhanek 2002; Milward 2005).

However, it is in the wider context that Beck (2000) identifies the risks related to the changing face of work, the workplace and culture. Organisational change is posited as a market response to wider changes in both home and global economies and in a service-driven economy which has largely rendered the idea of a 'job for life' redundant (Beck 2000; Senior 2002). As space, time and boundaries, such as those of the public and private, blur in a global economy, Beck's concern is that 'labour has become individualised' and 'local' with the consequence that risks are created for individuals around job stability (Beck 2000, 27–28). Beck (2000, 40) refers to the changing nature of work aligned with observable technological advances as an 'evolutionary leap' into what he determines as a 'second modernity' and which in process, mirrors the momentous transition from traditional society into Modernity. Beck (2000) argues that the diversity argues that the diversity and individualism that is a principle feature of this 'leap' will inevitably lead to the disintegration of society. This is, of course, at odds with the coherent, cohesive and hierarchical order that Weber attributed as necessary for bureaucratic order (1947). Individualisation, according to Beck (2000, 56) is underpinned through a process of 'internal globalisation' wherein, work tasks and interactive networks become decentralised and facilitated through a language of 'management speak' or predicated on jargonistic or 'enigmatic terms' which are 'developed in the social laboratory of management.

A Bureaucratic Affair

Beck's (2000, 56) observation has particular salience in relation to the organisational changes occurring in the UK's Civil Service. The Civil Service offers a fertile site for investigation as it not only embraces the management-speak of change strategies, such as HRM, but is necessarily aligned with furthering the cause of modernising government. The UK's Civil Service enjoys a worldwide reputation of high esteem and reform seeks to capitalise on this reputation and its tradition. Its rapid growth through the Nineteenth century necessitated a hierarchical structure which was based on standardised ways of working and which ensured parity across its many departments (Weber 1947; Drewry and Butcher 1991; Pyper 1995). The call for reform has, and remains, an ongoing project in the Civil Service initially in respect of standardisation and in more recent decades in respect of its efficiency and 'value for money' (Drewry and Butcher 1991; Dowding 1995; Pyper 1995).

Radical reform during the years of the Thatcher Government looked to 'downsize' its ever growing workforce and set about a process of 'hiving off' functions through the creation of quasi-independent agencies (Fry 1985; Drewry and Butcher 1991; Dowding 1995; Pyper 1995; Pilkington 1999). In 1999 the Blair Government launched its reform initiative, 'Modernising Government'. The three key aims of this White Paper centred on 'Delivery and Values' (Civil Service Reform: Delivery and Values Report, 2004:7, 1, 10). Critical of previous reform that had plunged Civil Service morale to an all time low, this reform shifted away from an emphasis around issues of economy and efficiency, to instead take a long-term view, that revolved around quality of service (Modernising Government 1999:6,1). Raising Civil Service morale alongside long-term reform called for a complementary strategy that ensured business objectives but at the same time valued the skills and talents of civil servants. HRM as a strategy for change was deemed to meet this twofold challenge. However little research exists around how civil servants experience change or the discourse of management strategies such as HRM and this case study set out to redress that imbalance.

Internal Corridors

Most research in the Civil Service is internally conducted through the Home Office. My requests to carry out an ethnographic exploration of the effectiveness of change communication were approved if I could ensure anonymity of the research field. Accordingly the research field will, from now, be referred to as 'The Department'. A triangulated approach considered change in 'The Department' from several directions. It first took a wide approach that looked at The Blair Government's reform initiatives; it then considered how reform impacted on departmental policy; how this was then communicated through 'The Department's' intranet site and finally through the interpretations, experiences and voices of its civil servants.

Approximately forty-eight civil servants worked in a selected division in 'The Department'. Assured of anonymity and confidentiality, a snowball sample totalling twenty-four participants from the division took part in this case study. Ranging in age from twenty-two to fifty-six years of age and comprising of eleven females and thirteen males, these civil servants had worked in 'The Department' between two and thirty years and, in a hierarchical grade structure were, proportionally representative of clerical and managerial grades. Over a period of fourteen months data was collected by means of observation, semi-structured interview, conversation, and through secondary sources such as the intranet.

HRM as a Strategy

It quickly became apparent that the mechanism for change in 'The Department' was its HRM strategy. Contemporarily HRM as we know it today was formerly referred to as 'Personnel Management' (Legge 1995; Mabey et al. 1998). However we need to distinguish between HRM as responsible for personnel function and HRM as a strategy that focuses on achieving managerial objectives (Guest 1987; Storey and Sissons 1993; Mullins 2002). Generally two models of HRM strategy are identified;

a 'hard' model defined as a 'utilitarian instrumental' approach usually associated with the manufacturing industry and, a 'soft' model defined as 'developmental humanist' in approach (Legge 1995; Dickens 1998; Mabey et al. 1998).

A 'soft' humanist model values employees and their creative talents as valuable assets which are instrumental in achieving an organisation's success (Legge 1995; Mabey, et al. 1998). This approach recognises the skills, quality output and commitment of workers as competitively advantageous and invests in nurturing and developing worker adaptability and commitment through collaborative opportunities (Legge 1995; Dickens 1998). The varying models of HRM as a strategy are founded on the integration of an organisation's policies, systems and activities. The 'hard' model of HRM, determines humans as an economic resource while the 'soft' model is person-centred, focusing on developing a resourceful skilled workforce that is highly committed to achieving organisational goals and objectives (Legge 1995; Dickens 1998; Mabey, et al. 1998). As a strategy then, the effectiveness of HRM relies on harnessing worker commitment toward a common goal but first the discourse of integration and commitment has to be communicated effectively. Determining which model of HRM strategy 'The Department' utilises is problematic. Initially it could be identified as person centred in approach and thereby a 'soft' model. However, in other respects the hierarchical structure and tradition of standardised working practices in the Civil Service makes it difficult to fully embrace the creative and empowering discourse of the person centred approach. Necessarily it relies on functionally maintaining order across its disparate departments and this lends itself toward a 'hard' model of HRM which highlights Legge's (1995) point that determining models of HRM strategy can be difficult and 'The Department' is no exception in this respect.

The Department's Discourse of HRM

It soon became apparent that 'The Department's' HRM strategy was the driving force of its reform. A force that operationally ensured quality service would be achieved within an integrated framework and that clearly determined a discourse of 'professionalism' around 'The Department's' expectations of how staff should conduct 'The Department's' everyday business. A clearly identifiable discourse of professionalism is embedded and underpins 'The Department's' HRM strategy and ways of working. However, having said that, it is arguable that this is not a new concept but simply a way of identifying or 'branding' existing work practices at the researched site in question. The site in question has a reputation for its delivery and professionalism and as the data will reveal while some of the civil servants positively embrace the concept of professionalism in their everyday discourse, the ways in which this is achieved is often disregarded or given scant attention.

A clear way to gain staff support of a new initiative is to include them in the decision making process and in respect of its HRM strategy, 'The Department' has taken an active lead in encouraging its people to attend and contribute to its ethos through internal workshops. The implication here is that it is a shared strategy which is not static but evolving. In many respects the key ingredients of 'The Department's' strategy have been evolving for a number of years. For example, the integration of the organisation's policies (Dickens 1998) can be seen as evident in such processes as its performance review procedures which in turn is a mechanism for determining an individual's eligibility for a salary increase or promotion.

Integration of an organisation's policies is first underpinned through its mission statement, aims, goals, and objectives. Clarity in this respect then determines and cascades the ethos of an organisation's business objective, albeit that, at first sight the aims and objectives can seem somewhat generalised. 'The Department' is no exception in this respect and its goals and objectives are similar to many other government departments or large organisations. In the interests of 'The Department's' anonymity specific wording has been obscured but at the heart of its business objective 'The Department' like many organisations advocates it will; 'secure people with the right skills to deliver its services', 'enhance and utilise the skills of its people', 'seek to improve and manage its performance' and, 'to enhance its culture'. As the goals cascade down the organisation's hierarchy they diversify still further into a set of 'behaviours' such as 'we embrace challenge and innovation', 'we are committed to making a difference',' we seek to learn and improve' and in common with many other organisations 'we value openness and honesty'.

'The Department's' Behaviours

It is these 'behaviours' that from a bottom-up perspective impact into the reporting system and become measurable in respect of performance pay. The civil servants throughout the reporting year are charged with collecting a portfolio of evidence that support how operational task objectives have been met and interestingly, in a hierarchical grade structure, it was noticeable that many of the civil servants in the administrative and lower managerial grades were acutely aware how the 'behaviours' informed or fitted into the performance reporting system. Conversely, and perhaps not surprisingly, at a higher managerial level civil servants, focused more specifically on operational aspects of their duties with little regard around how the integrated nature of the 'behaviours' affected them or indeed, their staff on whom they must subsequently report.

The integrated nature and wider vision of 'The Department's' HRM strategy is not perhaps immediately apparent but its discourse is prominent and as the reporting system illustrates its significance albeit at an instrumental level has relevance to some of its civil servants. The 'behaviours' are a good illustration around how effective 'The Department' is in disseminating the discourse of its HRM strategy. The goals, objectives and 'behaviours' are prominently publicised on the intranet, stationery and so on. Yet while some instrumentally identify with these, others do not. When Fred was asked if he was familiar with 'The Department's' goals and objectives, he replied, 'yes and no. I have read bits about delivering results and, but it doesn't really mean anything to me'. Fred was not alone in this comment; similar comments suggested 'it really doesn't affect me' and in several instances civil servants suggested that these were defined for those employees who were in the 'front line' that is, those dealing face to face with the general public or, those civil servants whose existing performance was raising concerns. In this instance it is questionable whether 'The Department's' HRM strategy and its discourse is making itself heard.

Keith acknowledged that he knew of the goals and objectives but was cynical around 'The Department's' motive and in particular, its 'behaviours'. He said,

> I see where they are coming from and I see what they are trying to do but I think they don't necessarily mean anything to the common man. What's the latest one about nine things that we do now, we are open and honest and all that sort of stuff.

Similarly, Sara agreed with this sentiment and had reassured her team that she did not 'want anybody worrying they are going to trip themselves up and fall over' because she knew that they were 'adhering to the standards and behaviours'. The behaviour that caused the most comment was that of being 'open and honest'. Typically when this behaviour was mentioned civil servants concurred with Keith when he said, 'So now we are open and honest and before we weren't I presume?'

Without doubt, some of the discourse around the behaviours did cause offence and was seen as patronising as the above examples illustrate. Overall the impression given by the cohort as a whole was that aside from the instrumental use of the 'behaviours', they were 'common sense' and had little relevance to the work being undertaken in the 'division'. Matt best summed this up when he commented,

> the people who work here are very switched on. I don't think they need to be pushed in any of these areas. They live those values rather than have to be promoted, they don't need to be told or guided, they live the values.

Finally lack of credence was further illustrated by Ian's comment; 'Personally you know I think they (the behaviours) are a bit wacky, daft'.

'The Department's' HRM strategy is clearly intent on modernising government through quality service and so on, but as the above quotes illustrate if the message of its discourse is seen as patronising or irrelevant then it becomes risky around its impact and effectiveness. We also need to bear in mind several other related points that are unique to the Civil Service and its culture. First it has a legacy of reform dating back over one hundred and fifty years, a legacy that is reinforced by negative media coverage and stereotypical images. More recently, reform has significantly reduced the number of civil servants and morale as the Prime Minister Mr Blair, identified has been rendered at an all time low. While the discourse of HRM holds promise of a brighter future organisationally and individualistically there also exists a lack of confidence around its effectiveness. Largely because it comes at the end of a long line of strategies; strategies which elicited comments such as, 'we've heard it all before', 'it's the latest fad' and so on. Indeed, many of the civil servants when referring to the latest fad or 'today's buzz words', reeled off previous initiatives and strategies that they had experienced. Examples included; 'Total Quality Management', 'Investors in People' and, 'Human Resource Development'.

Another key point to consider is the uniqueness of its history, a history predicated on the fundamentals of standardisation. Metaphorically it could be described as a 'bureaucratic machine' and indeed many times reference was made to the site as a 'clerical factory'. This mechanistic tradition is distinct from the private sector where business strategies are more easily applied (Seifert and Tegg 1998; Brown 2004). The spirit of enterprise generated by the Thatcher Government clearly set the scene for embedding a business ethos. But while the Civil Service is used to quickly responding to the demands of changing governments and their respective policies, the expectation is that it does so alongside the latest business strategies or initiatives. It is the succession of such initiatives that, civil servants negatively recognise as 'the latest fad' and which negate the discursive effectiveness of 'The Department's' HRM strategy. Indeed, this apparent civil servant cynicism toward 'management speak' echoes Beck's (2000) concern around the wider possibility of a breakdown in cohesion and order. Such cynicism then holds the potential to create risk at a macro level both in respect of 'The Department's' current HRM strategy but also, the subsequent initiatives that will undoubtedly follow. We will return to this point at a later stage but first we need to explore how a discourse of HRM creates everyday risks for individuals.

Everyday Risky Consequences

The discourse of HRM and 'professionalism' is best understood from a bottom-up approach. That is through the everyday experiences and risks that affect 'The Department's' civil servants. Three key themes emerged from the data that hold the potential of risk for individuals; team/family identity, perceptions of work-life balance and risky commitment.

Team/Family Identity

Building on previous initiatives the workforce strongly identify with teamwork. The cohort, work within a 'division' of 'The Department' and for the most part, the division breaks down into smaller teams. Interestingly the discourse of 'The Department's' 'behaviours' determines a shared ownership, for example, 'we will be open and honest', clearly is intended to pick up on the concept of teamwork and shared responsibility. While the discourse of HRM advocates realising and releasing the potential of individuals and their respective skills, it does so in the context of civil servants being a valuable asset to their team.

Ezzy (2001) likens teamwork to the notion of a pseudo-family and in this respect it becomes a powerful tool with which to engineer or re-engineer a work culture. By drawing an analogy between team and family structure, Ezzy (2001) suggests a culture can be engineered to socialise individuals into a shared sense of responsibility. Simplistically as social actors we learn to differentiate our loyalties and identity with the beliefs and values of our family. Social learning ensures that to varying extents we learn to comply, conform and potentially obey the rules of our family and our worldview is constructed based on these learned beliefs and values. Underlying this familial relationship is commitment. Ezzy identifies that this process of familial identification and commitment similarly can be applied in the workplace via team working. The suggestion is then that a discourse of teamwork is interchangeable with that of the family and alongside that the notion of team responsibility and commitment holds the potential to become self-policing.

Engaged in evaluating a service provided to internal customers, Ian's comments go some way to illustrate this point and his sense of team loyalty and pride:

> When I did my research the responses to the questions about my team were always more positive than the responses to the question about the organisation or division. Because my team are my friends and my family and we do everything pretty well, ... Don't we everyone? So I will give you an eighty-five. The rest of the division and all the other sides, not so good and 'the Department' very poor.

The civil servants slipped easily between pronouns as they described situations of 'us' and 'them'. At times the 'them' represented 'The Department' itself as an entity, external customers, colleagues within the same division and managers; sometimes their own team leader who located alongside the team were sometimes one of 'us' and at other times one of 'them' depending on the context being referred to. The analogy between pseudo-family and team was most apparent when somebody let the team down, whether that be a team member of the same grade, team leader or a divisional colleague. This sometimes created a sense of disappointment or of lost opportunity, an emotive response that befitted a family rather than a professional setting. As a self-policing mechanism while it illustrates the calculating nature of engineering a culture it also highlights the potential everyday risk for individuals should they let their team or pseudo-family down.

Good teams, like secure families, are made up of individuals with complementary and diverse, skills and strengths. The discourse of HRM encourages individuals to release their own potential and therein become empowered. To that end civil servants can opt for job related training and are encouraged to expand their skills and creativity. The problem with this is that often individuals are just too busy to take up such opportunities and this creates everyday risk. Risk that individuals are not up to date in their knowledge or approach to work which potentially could later impact not just on their team (or pseudo-family) but also on the individual's performance review. For example, Penny who was approximately forty-five to fifty years old said,

> I think you get to a certain age and think, I don't want to be developed or challenged any more ... the opportunities are there and they wouldn't stop me but as I say at my age .... I'm sure they would support me but I don't need to. I will save the money and give it to somebody else, let somebody else do it.

The everyday risk that Penny or individuals like her, may experience is that she may be perceived as being disinterested. Penny was not alone in her approach to her job, several civil servants both female and male expressed the view that they had been developed enough and were safe in the knowledge they did a good job and just wanted to work their allotted hours for which they received adequate remuneration. On the face of it this could be construed as lacking ambition, motivation and so on and there are potential consequences of this financially in respect of performance reviews and also the perception of team members around whether someone is taking full responsibility within the team around their contribution. For example, empathically individuals on several occasions were referred to as not being very good at something but it was 'OK because one of us prefers or has the skills for that task'. This is all well and good if the family (or team) are on good terms but if the familial relationship is fractious then therein is the potential for everyday risk around someone's suitability or efficiency. Another risk around a pseudo-family arrangement is that annoying habit of family members speaking for you and this was the case with one manager when talking about a member of her staff, who said,

> she's like me, same age as me. She's probably ... (pause) ... if she needs training ... (pause) ... she will do it but we tend to ... (pause) ... you know training on the job sort of thing.

The risk here raises the question, who is it that is reluctant to undertake training; is it the staff member or is it perhaps the manager? It could represent a true picture of both women or given the narrative pauses, it could also simply be a matter of the manager projecting her own reticence. As this theme illustrates there is considerable potential for everyday risks around team or family affiliation and commitment. As a self-policing mechanism such a collectivity works well and the discourse of HRM perpetuates this notion of family through its prevalent use of the pronoun 'we'. Its 'behaviours', 'we are honest and open', exemplify this.

Perceptions of Work-Life Balance

This relationship between a pseudo-family/team is of course, not a new one in the civil service and culturally dates back to 1919 and Warren Fisher who formerly as Head of the Civil Service was highly instrumental in organising social events. The notion of family is well established across the researched site and the many job losses incurred at this site seem to have embedded the protective nature of the family still further within its culture. The tradition of social interaction through social events has continued although contemporarily to a much lesser extent. The nature of HRM and level of organisational commitment shown in respect of long hours has created everyday risks around skewed 'work-life balance'. While the discourse of HRM strives for organisational commitment, the integrated nature of its policies also includes its 'work-life' balance initiative. While some of the cohort had heard of this others had not. Frank who had vaguely heard of it said:

> I wouldn't even know what the work-life balance initiative is supposed to mean for me frankly. I know that there are reams of paper and reams of words on the intranet but I mean realistically work-life balance is supposed to mean be gentle with yourself, and it's garbage.

Frank explained that in addition to the duties on his job description many more tasks had been 'dropped on' him at short notice; he suggested that, 'Wishful thinking that's what I understand by it. The idea of work-life or what work-life balance means is just pie in the sky'.

The everyday risk here is clearly around emotional and physical well-being. The data indicated that individuals demonstrated their organisational commitment by working in excess of their hours and were prepared to flexibly work late in order to meet business objectives and last minute requests. However, In respect of work-life balance and organisational commitment, in addition to an imbalance around emotional or physical well-being, a further associated risk exists. Clive reported,

> I have never been very good at that (work-life balance). I get into trouble for, one of the other staff, I sometimes get told off about that. But yes I have to be a little careful sometimes with that.

As far as domestic responsibility would allow, staff would inconvenience themselves to meet deadlines and demonstrate their flexibility and organisational commitment in this respect. Several civil servants seemed to see this as a trade off; a practical way of demonstrating commitment that due to domestic responsibility or work-balance concerns, they were unable or unwilling to demonstrate in other ways. For example, a number commented that because of domestic responsibility or because they wished to work traditional '9 to 5' (or comparable) hours this then eliminated them from pursuing their career to the next level. Considerable justification accompanied these comments around making 'choices' between career and family or leisure pursuits. These individuals recognised that the higher they climbed up the grade structure the more vulnerable they became to a mobile posting that could see them relocated or travelling to meetings at the other end of the country. Poignantly the comment was made several times that perception of this initial choice determined or assumed a career identity that lacked aspiration. This raised concerns around the viability of resurrecting career aspirations at a later date.

What becomes evident is that as a business strategy, HRM, creates everyday risks both for the individual and the organisation. Its discourse creates opportunity but within that opportunity there also exists risk; the risk that individuals who do not 'get with the programme' or the discourse of HRM suggest a lack of organisational commitment which threatens perception of an individual's corporate identity.

Risky Commitment

Beck (2000) determined that the general move toward individualisation in society is similarly reflected in the workplace manifesting in various ways and inevitably producing risks. Contemporarily business strategy has embraced individualism and in a genre that seeks 'recipe like' solutions (Collins 1998), literature abounds with strategy and 'quick fix' remedies that embrace the reflexive practice of individualism. HRM is no exception in this respect particularly when a soft or person-centred model is adopted. Beck (2000, 56) determined that an inner globalisation has occurred which is wrapped up in management speak 'developed in the social laboratory of management'. The apparent person centred HRM model embraced by 'The Department' is just such a strategy and its discourse pervades its organisational structure. In the Blair Government's drive to 'Modernise Government' a discourse of 'professionalism' is prevalent throughout 'The Department' for example, via its intranet system, on its stationery and necessarily, applied through its performance appraisal system. The workforce clearly identifies with this concept, but cynicism creeps in through the actual process of how professionalism is achieved and this is particularly apparent in their dissent around the related 'behaviours'. These 'behaviours' although in this instance are embedded in 'The Department's' HRM strategy pervasively typify a 'management speak' that is both recurrent and symbolic of former initiatives

The integrated nature of HRM necessarily determines that the business objectives of an organisation are effectively communicated to the workforce driven through organisational policies and practices. However, as the data illustrates the extent to which policy and practice or at least awareness of these, speak to each other is questionable.

'The Department's' strategy at one level is highly individualistic. In practice its discourse affects all staff and yet many in the cohort do not seem to recognise its significance. The exception being a small core of individuals at the lower end of the grade structure who recognise its instrumental value in respect of performance related pay. Aside from this, the underpinning set of 'behaviours' were generally considered to be already existing common sense values that were embodied through everyday working practices. Dissemination of these were generally considered to be unnecessary and in some instances such as being 'open and honest' as patronising around existing work practices. 'The Department's' discourse of HRM also relies on effective team working which is family-like. Ezzy (2001) determines that there is distinct organisational advantage in engineering a pseudo-familial relationship because in doing so, individuals emotively enter into a complex process of socialisation and commitment which inevitably demands compliance through to obedience of group norms or, suffer the penalty of internal self-policing.

In respect of 'getting with the programme' individuals are expected to take responsibility for their own behaviour and their place in the organisation and ownership of team or familial values is clearly evident through the data. The discourse of empowerment and professionalism pervades the organisation. In this respect it is difficult for individuals to ignore its corporate identity. To openly do so positions an individual's identity as oppositional and there are everyday risks attached to this, not least of which is family (or team) discontent through to the material consequences of the performance related pay and promotion systems. Legge (1995) determined that HRM is difficult to define and 'The Department's' strategy affirms this.

Conclusion

Operationally and culturally there is a powerful interaction between old and new ways of working in 'The Department' which from a meso level makes the introduction of strategies such as HRM all the more difficult. Its history is predicated on a hierarchical and bureaucratic order (Weber 1947). Despite diversionary processes of 'hiving off', this order is still in place and drives the bureaucratic social coherence of the vast institution that is the Civil Service and which shoulders the immense responsibility of underpinning the business of government. While a discourse of HRM advocates individualism it does so within this framework and creates a schizophrenic persona that attempts to merge old and new ways of working. This highlights the point that Mabey et al. (1998:37) made that elements of HRM are not new but simply a fusing together of ideas that 'wrap around' and explain organisational change.

In this respect what needs to be remembered is that Civil Service reform has been an ongoing project for over one hundred and fifty years (Drewry and Butcher 1991; Pyper 1995) and HRM as a transformatory mechanism for change, actually wraps around many of its existing good practices. The reticence or disregard that the cohort, in general, demonstrated toward what they perceive as yet another strategy suggests that they are suffering 'initiative fatigue'. However, in some respects the discourse of HRM for example, around 'professionalism' has been appropriated within the everyday narrative of the cohort. The effectiveness of 'The Department's' strategy in this respect would positively suggest then, that a 'drip drip' effect around the 'branding' of existing practices is in evidence. However, therein, lays several risks. If the individual is not identifying with the strategy then it calls into question the effectiveness of the organisation's communication practices. If the individual is not identifying with the strategy's objectives and adopts an oppositional identity position then there are risks around potential material consequences. Finally, further risk can occur if the organisation is seduced by the power of strategies such as HRM and ignore the possibility that there formulation simply 'wraps around' established ways of working.

To be overzealous in assuming that public administration can operate in the same way as private enterprise ignores several key factors. First it overlooks the size of the Civil Service and the effect this has on responding to the rapidity of emergent business initiatives and strategies. And importantly, the drive to 'modernise government' must cautiously consider and adhere to its mantra of valuing its 'people', their existing skills and expertise. Prime Minister Blair advocated that 'modernising government' would be considered a long term project and clearly HRM takes centre stage in this pursuit. To avoid negative or indeed, apathetic responses, a substantial period of time needs to elapse to establish 'The Department's' HRM strategy at the fundamental core of its business and identity. Everyday risks are common place for today's civil servants as their professional commitment is tried and tested through the ever more complex demands of a modernising government. The introduction of new strategies from the private sector at this point would only run the risk of exacerbating existing 'initiative fatigue' still further.

References

Beck, U. (2000), *The Brave New World of Work* (Cambridge: Polity Press).
Brown, K. (2004), 'Human Resource Management in the Public Sector', *Public Management Review*, 6:3, 303–9.
Civil Service Reform (2004), 'Delivery and Values' Report (2004:7, 1.10) www. civilservice.gov.uk/reform/documents/delivery.values.pdf accessed 24 January 2005.
Collins, D. (1998), *Organisational Change: Sociological Perspectives* (London: Routledge).
Coulson-Thomas, C. (1997), *The Future of the Organisation* (London: Kogan Page).
DeCenzo, D. A. and Silhanek, B. (2002), *Human Relations; Personal and Professional Development* 2nd Edition (New Jersey: Prentice Hall/Pearson Education Ltd).
Dickens, L. (1998), 'What HRM means for Gender Equality', *Human Resources Management Journal* 8:1, 23–40.
Dowding, K. (1995), *The Civil Service* (London: Routledge).
Drewry, G. and Butcher, T. (1991), *The Civil Service Today* 2nd Edition (Oxford: Blackwell).
Edwards, P. J. and Bowen, P. (2002), *Risk Management in Project Organisations* (Oxford: Butterworth and Heineman).
Ezzy, D. (2001), 'A Simulacrum of Workplace Community: Individualism and Engineered Culture', *Sociology* 35, 631–50.
Fone, M. and Young, P. C. (2005), *Managing Risks in Public Organisations* (Leicester: Perpetuity Press).

Fry, G. K. (1985), *The Changing Civil Service* (London: George Allen and Unwin).

Guest, D. E. (1987), 'Human Resource Management and Industrial Relations', *Journal of Management Studies* 24:5, 503–21.

Kahneman, D. and Tversky, A. (1984), 'Choices, Values and Frames', *American Psychologist* 39, 341–50.

Legge, K. (1995), *Human Resource Management: Rhetorics and Realities* (Basingstoke: Palgrave).

Lupton, D. (1999), *Risk and Sociocultural Theory* (Cambridge: Cambridge University Press).

Mabey, C. et al. (eds) (1998), *Strategic Human Resource Management* (London: Sage Publications).

Millward, L. (2005), *Understanding Occupational and Organizational Psychology* (London: Sage).

Modernising Government (1999), 'Modernising Government', http://www.archive. officialdocuments.co.uk/document.cm43/4310/431sm.htm accessed 24 January 2005.

Mullins, L. J. (2002), *Management and Organisational Behaviour* 6th Edition (London: Prentice Hall Financial Times).

Pilkington, C. (1999), *The Civil Service in Britain Today* (Manchester: Manchester University Press).

Pyper, R. (1995), *The British Civil Service* (London: Prentice Hall/Harvester Wheatsheaf).

Reason, J. (1997), *Managing the Risks of Organisational Accidents* (London: Ashgate).

Seifert, R. and Tegg, V. (1998), 'Management Development in the British and Irish Civil Services', *Journal of Management Development* 17:9, 686–98.

Senior, B. (2002), *Organisational Change* (London: Prentice Hall).

Storey, J. and Sisson, K. (1993), Managing Human Resources and Industrial Relations (Buckingham: Open University Press).

Weber, M. (1947), *The Theory of Social and Economic Organisation*, trans. A. M. Parsons and T. Parsons (New York: Free Press).

Chapter 8

'Are We There Yet?' Negotiating Transitions and Meaning Crisis in Young Adults

Julie Scott Jones

Introduction

The life course to an extent used to be marked by rites of passage, both formal and informal (whether secular or religious), that moved us inexorably from childhood, through to adulthood (Van Gennep 1977; Bell 1997). This movement was usually associated with the gaining of various forms of status, influence and perhaps power within families, communities and other social spheres. Most importantly of all it could be seen as a process with structure and meaning, albeit contested meanings in many cases. Each stage had meanings, requirements, appropriate behaviours and responsibilities. This is not to suggest that the life course has been a historically or culturally fixed progress for the individual. As has been well documented (see for example Aries 1996; Stone 1980; Riley and Waring 1988; Vincent 2003) our views of and the meanings we attach to childhood, adulthood, and the aging process in general, have altered significantly through history. This can be seen most pertinently in the case of childhood, with the emergence and the idealisation of childhood in the Victorian era (Aries 1996).

Pre-modern societies with their fixivity, discourses that equated age with wisdom, and status hierarchies based on religion-infused epistemologies progressed people along the life-course with relative ease (Stone 1980; Aries 1996; Bell 1997). People knew they had a 'place', both in a socio-economic sense but also in an ontological sense. The means to attain that place were, typically, clearly marked out and structures were in place to facilitate progress, for example, through marriage (Bell 1997; Stone 1980; Newman and Gauerholz 2002). The shift into modernity may have disrupted some of the religious markers of adulthood, but many remained valid (for example marriage), and others were created (for example wage-earning). Most importantly of all, perhaps, the presumption remained that there was an adult world, with incumbent rights, responsibilities and behaviours, and a non-adult world characterised by a freedom and innocence of such trappings (Bell 1997; Newman and Gauerholz 2002). Being 'adult' was not just defined in economic terms, which became more prominent in modernity, but encompassed a broader sense of identity and meaning.

The emergence of childhood (Aries 1996) as a delineated stage of maturation (in a social sense) if anything exacerbated the adult-ness of the adult world. Therefore both pre-modernity and modernity offered some degree of ontological security to young adults. Of course, young adulthood[1] has always been a stage of insecurity, anxiety, transition: of finding one's place in the world of adults. However, it will be argued in this chapter that in contemporary society young adulthood is much more problematic, contested and inherently risky than in any previous era due to the shift into late modernity.

Poststructuralist sociology identifies contemporary society as being in 'late modernity' (Foucault 1984); a time of transition from the norms and certainties of modernity. Foucault (1984) viewed it as a period where individuals become reflexive (or 'knowing') enough to dissect, interrogate and challenge modernity's verities. Both Giddens (1990) and Beck (1994) echo this view that reflexivity becomes an ever more common aspect of self-identity, but also a strategy for constructing meaning systems (typically self-focused). In the absence of modernity's dominant Grand Narratives, institutions, traditions, obligations and securities, the individual becomes unanchored from previous communal identities and is forced to construct self-identity from whatever resources emerge (Giddens 1991). In addition, this shift into late modernity also forces the individual into an existential search for meaning, something that Berger identifies as 'the homeless mind' phenomenon (Berger et al 1974). Thus, late modernity is also an era where 'meaning crisis' is commonplace. This self-actualisation and search for meaning feed off of each other and work to make late modernity a period where risk discourses predominate (Giddens 1990; Beck 1992). Individuals are left alone to negotiate through such discourses and to try to work out a hierarchy of significances and meanings (Lupton and Tulloch 2002). Therefore it should be expected that 'adulthood' has become a much more fluid and contested life-stage within late modernity. Young adulthood has always been about a process of becoming and so we should always expect to see it associated with some sort of ontological insecurity. However it will be argued in this chapter that specific socio-economic trends exacerbate what might be termed the 'typical' ontological insecurities of the young adult. One might associate the worries, fear and frustrations of the young adults featured in this chapter as a normal part of the maturation process: the typical anxieties of those in a state of becoming. Yet these young adults are in a process that lacks the structure, certainties, traditions, and meanings of the past. How they negotiate this process, and the specific risks involved, are the focus of this chapter.

---

1 'Young adult' is here defined as an individual between the ages of eighteen and thirty who still has some degree of socio-economic dependency on family or other social support agencies. Such dependency is increasingly 'normalised' as part of this life-stage, but would be seen as increasingly abnormal post-thirty.

Methodological Information

This research draws on data collected over a four year period. The data was collected using informally structured focus groups of six to eight people. All the participants were final year university students studying Social Science or Humanities subjects at two large urban universities in the United Kingdom. The focus groups were run several times during the academic year. Each year a different cohort participated with a total of four cohorts involved. The students were all volunteers who were recruited via personal contact with the researcher. Their two requirements had to be a general interest in issues around adulthood and a willingness to self-reflect. As the students got used to the focus group forum and got to know each other, informal discussions would continue outside of the group and often students would bring comments or observations to the next meeting. It was quite clear that focus group discussions sparked wider debates between the participants and their friends who were not in the group. Again, participants would often discuss these subsequent conversations if they deemed them to be useful or insightful. Often subsequent focus group work would start with a student raising a point that had emerged from discussing group themes with friends.

Focus groups were chosen as they offer the 'opportunity to study the ways in which individuals collectively make sense of a phenomenon and contrast meanings around it'. (Bryman 2001, 338). Additionally, focus groups allow participants to define and attach meanings to what they consider important aspects of a subject. Participants can also challenge each other and the facilitator, much more than in conventional face-to-face interviewing (Bryman 2001). Each focus group ran for around two hours at a time. The researcher acted as 'facilitator' and started each with a general question or comment on adulthood, social trends, or more generally on the meaning of life. The whole group had an opportunity to comment in turn and then a discussion would develop. The researcher worked as facilitator of the discussion, but typically tried to step back and let the discussions continue.

Focus group data was collected via written notes and audio recordings. Subsequent focus groups for each cohort would start with issues raised from the previous one. At the start of each academic year the focus group would be quite formal and structured, but then become more informal as the students got to know each other; this greatly aided discussion. It should be noted that as all the participants were Social Science or Humanities students they already had some awareness of the issues being explored in focus group, prior to the start of the research. Additionally, all the students showed a greater level of reflection and theoretical awareness (for example, they understood the concepts of late modernity and had some insight into the sociological debates around consumerism) of the issues than one would expect from a group not studying these subject areas. Obviously three of the cohorts have now graduated from university, while the fourth is approaching graduation. Contact, via email, has been maintained with approximately one third of the twenty-two students who have graduated, so that their post-graduation lives can continue to be charted. Contact with the rest has been lost.

There were a total of thirty participants all of whom were aged between twenty-one and twenty-four years. In each cohort there were some students who knew each other from being in the same university classes and a few were close friends (in one instance flat-mates). Reflecting the gender bias of the subjects they were studying, the majority of the participants were female, with only eleven males. Eight of the participants were British Asian; one was Black British, while the rest were White British. Of the Asian students, six were Muslim and two were Hindus: all of whom actively practised their respective faiths, although with varying degrees of commitment. Of the White students, all nominally labelled themselves 'Christian', but none of them actively practised this faith and none identified themselves as 'religious'. Although the majority of the White students self-identified as 'spiritual', two students professed to be atheists. Sam, the sole Black student, was a devout Christian who regularly attended a local charismatic church and was involved in faith healing, but preferred to self-define as 'spiritual' rather than as 'Christian'. None of the group were married, but most were in some form of semi-committed relationship, although few cohabitated with their partners. None of the group were parents, although one (Syed[2]) was about to become a father for the first time. Most of the group lived in rented student accommodation, although the majority of the Asian students still lived in their respective parental homes. Unsurprisingly, the entire group had some level of student debt, but none of them felt that the debt was above the average for a 'typical' university student today. In terms of class, all the students identified themselves as middle class, more specifically lower middle class, although most felt that class was a meaningless term as (in Kate's words):

> everyone's the same now … everyone has the same dream … it's like we all became middle class somewhere in the '80s or our parents did … so really does that mean class is now meaningless as an idea, I think so.

They were all as Parker described it 'true Thatcher's kids'. What he meant by that was that most of the students' families had become middle class 'suddenly' in the 1980s, as parents 'changed' from working class to middle class, typically but not exclusively, through home ownership. He also noted that their families were more preoccupied with their children's aspirations than in previous generations, and that there was pressure to 'do well' in studies, career and so forth. All the students were the first members of their families to attend university, which again demonstrates their families' transition into the aspirant middle classes (Goldthorpe et al. 1968; Roberts 2001).

---

2 Pseudonyms have been used to mask the identity of all research participants.

What Do You Want to be When You Grow Up?

In becoming adults, individuals typically assume or have ascribed to them specific statuses and responsibilities; as previously mentioned such statuses and responsibilities have changed over time and must also be culturally contextualised (Vincent 2003). A review of the changing meanings and definitions can be a useful starting point for exploration of adulthood today. Adulthood in the majority of communities through human history has been delineated by the related social statuses of spouse/parent (Bell 1997; Newman and Gauerholz 2002; Vincent 2003). In becoming husband/father or wife/mother one assumed a social status of some cultural significance. For women, especially, such statuses afforded value and influence, at least in the domestic sphere (Connell 2005). With the emergence of modernity, additional social roles have been added to that of 'adult', for example, employee/wage earner, voter, and tax payer; in other words full participant in civil and capitalist society. This particularly added to the worth of being an adult man. For women domestic-linked statuses remained more significant and meaningful (Connell 2005). However, the past thirty years has seen women, in particular middle class women, increasingly define adulthood in male terms associating it with career/wage earning; participation in higher education and home ownership. Significantly, economic and social trends of the past three decades have created a normative adult status that is overwhelmingly middle class, and that is defined by aspiration and acquisition (Roberts 2001):

Rhiannon summarised it succinctly:

> You get the grades, to get to Uni, to get the good degree, to get the good job, ... why? So you can have a nice house, car, holidays ... life. That's it, over and out the meaning of life in a few easy steps!

Rhiannon's mantra was one shared by all the participants in this study. Indeed it could be a summary of the markers of adulthood in the late modern era, driven by and feeding off of consumer society.

When asked the question 'describe what makes someone an 'adult' or what marks out an 'adult' today', the students invariably started by listing economic markers: graduate level job/career; home ownership; good disposable income; affluent, consumer lifestyle; having choices (possibly power) via economic means; job insecurity; and debt. When asked if adults have an automatically high social status the students identified economic clout as the only key status, acknowledging the decline in authority gained through age. Further exploration of the issue saw the students identifying a range of behaviours that were once adult-only, but could now be seen as common amongst teenagers and increasingly older children. These included, among others, sexual activity, alcohol consumption, drug misuse, swearing, and having legal rights. Thus these behaviours were not associated with being 'grown-up' by the students. When asked if being 'adult' brought with it responsibilities, respect or obvious authority, none of the students saw these as automatic aspects of adulthood that they should be granted or seek to develop. In their view, being 'adult' today is predominantly an economic status and therefore by its nature is somewhat precarious to obtain and maintain. If we look beyond this study at populist and academic debates on status and adulthood it too has a central focus on the economic (see for example Carpenter 2007). Contemporary educational and political discourses of achievement define it solely in terms of economic value and attainments, so no wonder then that the students in this group associate status with economic worth.

However as this definition of adulthood has developed; 'old' forms of being or marking out 'adult' would appear to be diminishing in significance, for example, marriage and parenthood. Key trends relating to marriage and parenthood suggest a more fluid and almost casual approach to both, for example, the decline in marriage itself and the rise in cohabitation with its higher incidence of break-up (ONS 2007). Serial monogamy dominates over lifelong monogamy. In relation to parenthood, especially among the middle classes, an increasing number avoid it altogether, while others delay it (ONS 2007). The age of first parenthood is now in the early thirties and getting older; a major shift over the past two decades (ONS 2007). All the participants, bar four, saw pursuing a 'meaningful' career, home ownership and a disposable income as 'being grown-up'. In contrast marriage was seen as 'past its sell-by date' (Dean); 'just a piece of paper' (Amy); and 'an empty ritual ... just an excuse for a do' (Jo). Parenthood was seen as 'something for the future ... once I've worked out my life..who I am ... get what I want' (Jo); something that could be postponed almost infinitely. The female participants, in particular, identified having a child as an obstacle to personal ambitions. However, some of the participants in this study rather than avoiding or dismissing traditional forms of adulthood, sought to embrace them as a means to define identity and status; a theme that will be explored later in this chapter.

More significantly is the fact that as this latest 'version' of adulthood has developed; the participants believe that the means to achieve it have reduced. The participants drew on media discourses about graduate unemployment, high property costs, the cost of living, the fertility 'timebomb' and the pensions crisis, to illustrate that growing up was hard to do and beset with risks that their parents might not have had to face. Beck (1992) identifies the media as key amplifiers of risk discourses, blowing social facts out of proportion in relation to their actual threat and significance. This media amplification means that individuals, who increasingly rely on the media for 'expert' knowledge, find it hard to perceive or contextualise the reality of the threat in question.

The students noted that the 'value' of a university degree has been diminished by the increasing number of graduates, caused by the very expansion of the universities and middle classes that had benefited their own families. All this was seen to have made the aspired for 'good job' harder to obtain. This particularly makes sense if we unpack what 'good job' is taken to mean both for individuals and how it is 'sold' to school-leavers and graduates via the current media and educational discourses. As Nisha explains:

> there are loads of jobs ... but who wants to do something in an office ... bored ... I want something that has meaning ... not like saving the world or anything over the top like that ... but something that challenges me, ... creative ... where I use my brain ... that's a good job.

Nisha's definition of a 'good' job was universally shared by all the participants. 'Good' job could be contrasted with the 'crap jobs' they all did to help fund their time at university.

Also, rising property prices, the increasing UK cost of living and so forth have meant that the 'shiny consumer dream' (as Joe described it) was increasingly seen as 'out of reach' or only reachable if one wishes to get into serious, perhaps lifelong, debt. One could perhaps view such unease as symptomatic of the in-transition status of university students or a case of pre-graduation 'jitters'. However, the participants were drawing on an interpretation, albeit a particularly gloomy one, of current economic statistics and realities, as well as more populist discourses in the media. Thus the current model of adulthood (as a set of economic markers) is increasingly problematic for the very individuals whom should assume it with relative ease: middle class university graduates. The decline in other markers of adulthood, for example, marriage or age based hierarchies, make this situation even more problematic as it removes alternative routes to adult status.

A Quick Word about Class

Class is clearly an issue when exploring discourses of adulthood. With middle class-ness almost meaningless in the face of embourgeoisment (Goldthorpe et al 1968) and middle class-ness as the current norm, then clearly those belonging to the working classes may struggle to make use of economic markers (home ownership, graduate level career etc.) of adult identity and may seek other means. Early parenthood, gang membership and other clearly 'risk-taking' strategies may be useful, if potentially stigmatising.[3] But then in a world where middle class-ness is a normative value status, being working class itself already brings with it a certain degree of stigma (for an exploration of some of these issues see Skeggs 1997; McRobbie 2004; McDowell 2006). However for the middle classes such obvious risky adult-defining strategies would be disastrous in relation to long-term social status. How then do they negotiate adulthood, when the markers of adulthood are increasingly difficult for them to attain? Do they pursue the late modern version of adulthood with its 'risks' of debt, a mundane job, and the meaninglessness of consumerism or 'risk'

---

3 See Merryweather and Laverick in this volume for examples of working class construction of identity.

remaining in a sort of state of 'becoming', of transition which lacks boundaries, status and is characterised by potential meaning crisis? And what of those more traditional markers of adulthood, such as marriage and parenthood, how do they fit into this pattern of 'deferred' adulthood?

A Funny Thing Happened on the Way to Adulthood...

Just as the markers of adulthood have changed so the participants also identified that adulthood had appeared to have fragmented. They identified an increasing trend towards people in their twenties, thirties and possibly early forties acting 'like big teenagers' (Meera). Cameron summed up the general view of most of the students; that increasingly the distinctions between the grown-ups and the children were becoming blurred:

> What is grown up today ... I mean how is it marked? Kids and adults both binge drink ... no one respects authority ... in fact authority, deference, any notion of age equals seniority is out ... laughed at ... you've got these thirtysomethings going to 'school disco' nights and students wearing Girl Guide t-shirts, and everyone's trying to look young and cool and trendy and I'm like fucking everyone just stop ... just fuckin' get your shit together and grow up.

This issue raised a debate about the so-called 'death of childhood' (see for example Palmer 2006), with the students viewing older children as acting like teenagers, while teenagers were basically treated like 'adults with acne' (Alexa). They highlighted that all age-groups now have legal rights and in a sense power, citing the example, of children having power over teachers by threatening to phone 'Childline', if they do not like them or their approach to punishment. Late modernity seems to represent a break from a discourse of linear progression through the life course; children can be adult-like and adults can be child-like. Given that late modernity is about the contestation of categories and the blurring of boundaries, perhaps, this is to be expected but it brings with it increased risks for all concerned, from child protection issues, to the consequences of this decline in adult authority. An example of the 'juvenilisation' of adulthood that the students kept citing was what might be termed the fetish for childhood-retro that has dominated all aspects of pop culture for the past decade. From Playstation games that hark back to childhood television shows such as *Knight Rider* and *Miami Vice*; to 'school disco' themed club nights; to clothes utilising childhood motifs, from Brownies to *Bagpuss*. The underlying theme is that adults are just 'big' kids out for hedonistic, albeit slightly more grown-up fun. Adulthood seems to lack authenticity, which are the 'really real' adults; no wonder the adults 'play kid' and the kids get to play 'adult'.

The students identified adulthood as having three potential stages: the first stage (to which they belonged) was 'somewhere between teenager and middle age'. This was a time of 'having fun (Nazia); 'no obvious responsibilities' (Matt); and 'avoiding growing up' (Alexa). This stage seemed to end somewhere in the late thirties. The second stage was identified as 'definitely grown-up' (Amy), and associated with what they termed 'middle age', starting in the forties and involving 'serious responsibilities' (Sara). 'Serious responsibilities' were identified as including, the raising of children, looking after elderly parents, taking your career seriously, and having a mortgage and other financial commitments. It was this stage where people might be viewed as adult and being due 'some respect' (Sam). The final stage was associated with 'the elderly', seemingly starting with retirement and ending with death. This stage was seen as one of decline, fear and 'not fun' (Sam). The participants in a sense were identifying a fragmentation of adulthood that is now starting to be explored theoretically within the Social Sciences (see for example Vincent 2003).

This 'deferred adulthood' has already been identified and labelled 'young adulthood' and many theorists have identified the prolonging of adolescence or at least the delaying of adulthood as a recent phenomenon (Vincent 2003; Furedi 2004). This 'new' stage of adulthood is caused by the socio-economic trends and risk discourses of late modernity. There is also the issue of dependency and risk-aversion. Furedi (2004) notes that increasingly we prolong young adult dependency on parents and that the more economic trends make them vulnerable to economic dependency the more familial dependency increases. Also, Furedi (2004) notes that 'therapy' culture avoids individuals taking responsibility for their own actions and risks, despite the fact that taking responsibility has always been associated with being an 'adult', thus this shift to dependency might have an impact on adult identity formation. Yet, ironically, 'therapy' culture encourages the confessional and the breaking down of barriers between individuals. In its most dramatic form we can see this in the daytime talk show genre, with the 'anything goes' airing of family secrets. All of the students, except the Asian ones, commented on the fact that they felt at times that parents tried to be friends 'too much' both in how they treated their children but also in the sharing of personal information. Examples of this were Claire's parents, separately, sharing information about their increasingly 'nasty' divorce, while Parker's mother confided in him details of her ongoing extra-marital affair. Again this echoes the blurring of boundaries between age groups that has been already discussed. Over protective parents, politicians and educators' risk aversive preoccupations have created in Generation Y,[4] young adults who are merely grown-up adolescents and less ontologically secure than past generations (Furedi 2004).

> Charlotte: My mum is great but she can't let go … she has to try and make sure everything's covered, safe … I could put up with that at school, but at Uni … she still thinks that she should fuss around and worry..but I want to be left to make my own mistakes and stuff … I don't need to be bubble-wrapped.

---

4 Today's Twentysomethings, sometimes also known as 'The Millennium Generation' or the 'Noughties' generation.

Yet ironically, many of the students also identified the comforting element of this over-protectiveness:

> Waheeda: I know that they [parents] want the best for me and know best ... I like that they try and control things ... its safe ...

> Cameron: It's this weird love/hate dependency ... like on the one hand you want them [parents] to step back and leave you to make mistakes ... but then you think ... shit ... can I really do this on my own ... there's this anxiety ...

Thus, the students in this study had both endured parents who had been preoccupied with risks, however remote, and thus had been over-protective, while at the same time experienced a lack of boundaries between grown-ups and children. The same parents who felt they could transgress boundaries by sharing 'adult' information with their children about divorces or affairs, would at the same time treat them as infants to be over-protected. Most of the students felt less prepared for adult life, but also felt an urge to embrace risks within it. In terms of self-actualisation this has created a profound conflict as the students found it harder to construct biographies independent of parental influence, when the very meaning of grown-up seems so meaningless. The following two quotes illustrate this phenomenon:

> Liz: I feel less confident about getting out there into like..you know..the big bad world. I don't necessarily think that I feel ready to make big decisions for myself ... without having my mum being there ... god that sounds really pathetic!

> Rea: ... who wants to be grown up today ... there's no respect anyway for adults ... I keep thinking when does it get to be my turn, when do they let me grow up ... but then I think who wants to be grown up anymore anyway ... it's just too much to deal with.

Life and Stuff

Being in your Twenties, for the middle classes at least, is increasingly more like a prolonged Gap Year between school and the 'real' world (read here grown-up world). Much of the populist focus on this generation has been on their perceived selfishness, self-preoccupation and their domination of popular cultural discourses. Yet this same group also live in a perpetual existential conflict, between 'playing the game' (Charlotte) or 'getting out' (Jo). As Steve put it, 'is crippling debt and no likelihood of your own home, really work sticking around for'. Similarly, this generation has been over-sold two powerful and unrealistic discourses: having it all is at your fingertips and you can do anything you want to do. The students in this study were aware of both discourses and felt let down that neither was realistic:

> Steve: Having it all is only for a few lucky people ... who really gets the great job ... the satisfying, creative career, and all that.

Consumerism, which could be identified as *the* belief system of late modernity is seductive in its discourse of 'choice' that is both tantalising (with its seemingly endless possibilities) and yet bewildering (with its lack of structure to frame such choices). The reflexivity of late modernity identified by Foucault (1984), Giddens (1990) and Beck (1992) also means that we can appreciate our lack of 'real' choice. As Nazia put it:

> the choice is between that dull job and that one, or that car rather than that car, the green iPod or the pink one ... these are all material choices ... they aren't permanent or meaningful.

Additionally, consumerism was seen as an 'empty' preoccupation:

> Cameron: it's totally fucked up ... buy this, buy that ... earn some more and you too can have more pointless fucking things in your house ... is that everything ... is that it ...god how depressing ... totally fucked up!

Adulthood is increasingly being defined in economic terms and is itself an increasingly fluid life-stage, especially at the early stage of young adulthood. Young adulthood seems to be a stage where there is a conflict between dependence and independence; an acknowledgment that the material world is devoid of meaning; and a realisation that 'full' adulthood may be decades away. Thus contemporary young adulthood is beset with a number of risks. The students in this study demonstrated a number of strategies that they use to negotiate this increasingly problematic world of 'deferred' adulthood. For the majority of them the risks lay not in challenging the system but in conformity to it: conformity was associated with their parents ('they're stuck or they can't see the bigger picture' – Rhiannon); and Baby Boomers ('weren't they the folk who have basically screwed everything up?' – Parker). The students were reflexive enough to see the 'bigger picture'; pessimistic about their chances of attaining the status and success markers they had been 'sold' as their route to success/personal fulfilment; did not consider themselves fully grown-up to deal with everything; and identified the lack of fulfilment or meaning in contemporary consumer society. All of them sought different routes, but all can be characterised by 'opting out' of certain late modern conformities, for example, consumerism. Four key strategies emerged from the group discussions, which will now be explored.

Keep on Moving

One of the most dominant discourses that emerged was that of travel and exploration and the need to do both: as Ally put it 'there's a big world out there'. Of the twenty-two graduates, seventeen had embarked on a period of independent travelling, following graduation. The typical backpacker routes of South East Asia and Australia were most popular. Escape and being able to 'delay the real world' (Jo) were the two most common reasons for travelling: travel has always been associated with both motives (Urry 2000; MacKenzie 2005; Walton 2005). But in addition travel was seen as a voyage of personal discovery and exploration: 'I want to find out who I am' (Shelley). 'I want to realise my limits and have thrills … adventure and not be safe … life is too safe.' (Matt). For Meera, the one Asian graduate who had embarked on a period of post-graduation travel, it was more fundamental than that:

> I wanted to finally do stuff separate from my family, to see what I can do and let them see that I don't need to be limited … that I can look after myself. It took me two years of negotiating with them to let me go … I was terrified that I would fuck things up and have to call home for help … that never happened.

Travel has long been a source of self-exploration, discovery and the development of 'adultness'; from the colonial adventuring of upper class men in the Victorian era to the spiritual searching of the counter-culture's trips to India. There is nothing new here in this sense. However what can be identified as new are two things. The first is deliberate thrill-seeking, not just through activities like bungee jumping or white water rafting, but through the desire to visit more 'risky', undiscovered countries.

> Cameron (on backpacking through South America): Everyone's done Thailand, Oz, India …I'm drawn to the new … the undiscovered … a little bit less safe … more risk … if I can come back from there … then that really says something about who I am.

Being able to 'rough it' and seek thrills echoes Lupton and Tulloch's (2002) contention that the more risk-avoidance discourses dominate, the more individuals seek deliberate risks as a form of rebellion and release.

> Claire: My life has seemed so charted out … school … Uni, degree, job, house, etc … I just want to get out there and where I can go … what I might find … the unknown is exciting.

An additional discourse that emerged was that of never-ending travel. Of the graduates, ten had returned to the UK only temporarily to raise funds for more travelling, in other words they were in a constant state of motion and none of them identified an end point.

> Luke: I look at home and see this … I guess rat race … and I think do I want to be one of those rats … in a shit job … earning money to buy shit I don't really need … is this it? I don't see why it has to be.

When asked about the risk of delayed entry into the jobs and housing markets, Luke replied:

> Yeah … you've got a point … but a bigger risk might be to just have your brain absolutely fucked over by staying put … being safe … I'd rather see the world and explore it while I can and not wake up one day and think shit, I've missed it all and for what … a big house and a car.

Of the students waiting to graduate, the majority also wished to travel for several years following graduation. They were not so much deferring adulthood as rejecting an economic model of it, which focuses mainly on acquisition and career building to further acquisition. In long-term travelling, the students were following a tried and tested route for self-responsibility, growth and meaning provision. Being 'out there' afforded self-actualisation, whereas being 'in there' merely stifled, repressed and controlled.

Making a Difference

As well as travel discourses, the other most powerful way of dealing with deferred adulthood was in seeking to 'make a difference'. This often went hand in hand with the travelling discourse. Of the thirty students in the sample, only Faz wanted to pursue a typical graduate fast-track career (in corporate finance). However, for the other students career ambitions were more about wanting to 'do good' and 'make a difference', through voluntary and ethically driven work. A strong ethical stance emerged around helping others both within the UK and in the rest of the world. A large number of the students who were long-term travellers worked, at least, temporarily on voluntary work overseas. There was a sense that the typical (read 'safe') graduate jobs of their peers, for example, teaching, social work and so forth were just 'unadventurous, safe, easy, dull, and more about paperwork than helping others' (Amy). There was also great cynicism about such careers:

> Sam: do they really ... really make a difference ... they're just doing those jobs cos they're safe, secure jobs ... they're not rushing to do them to change lives.

By 'making a difference' the students believed that they were gaining meaning and direction. They all also identified such jobs as hard to get or poorly paid, but that they were better 'risking it' and doing these jobs than 'being safe'. Such attitudes were also identified as being in direct conflict with parents:

> Alexa: My parents just don't seem to get it ... why you might actually want to do something other than just make money ... don't we have some sort of responsibility to others, to the future...beyond what's in it for us?

The over-protective parents who had controlled childhoods with strong risk-aversive discourses sought to continue their influence through 'safe' jobs discourses: 'my mother is always saying don't you want a nice job ... don't you want what everyone else has ... don't you want to be safe.' (Rea). There was also the 'risk' of letting parents down:

> Amy: I know my parents have worked hard to get themselves where they are today ... to do better than their parents and to get me to Uni. I do feel guilty that I'm not conforming to what they see as the good job, buy a house, have a nice life thing.

Many parents reacted to their children's non-conformity in a negative way:

> Claire: My mother is always trying to highlight the problems ... the dangers of me going
> to India [to do voluntary work] ... it's beyond manic with her ... sometimes I think ... it's
> a bit sinister ... like she's trying to control me ... she needs to let go ... I don't think parents
> today can let go that easily.

We can see this desire to 'make a difference' as partly the idealistic yearnings of
youth, which is certainly not unusual. However, the strength of the yearning to
'make a difference', while rejecting the 'safeness' of the typical graduate world
seems significant. Again, the risk is not in rejecting safeness but in accepting it. In
addition, the students showed a strong discourse of rebellion in their risk-adoption,
for them the desire to 'make a difference' contained within it a wider critique of what
they perceived to be late modernity's vacuous consumerism.

Embracing Old Ways of Being Grown-Up

The majority of the students were children of divorce, who had grown up with the
realities of lone parenthood or reconstituted families. In that sense they are typical of
their generation (Newman and Gauerholz 2002). This had instilled in most of them
two views: firstly that marriage or even long term cohabitation was not necessarily
a long-term goal and secondly a desire to avoid parenthood or at least to delay it.
Most of them challenged the inevitably of marriage and/or parenthood and did not
associate either with the increase of status or the assumption of adulthood. As Sam
notes:

> this dream of finding the ONE ... who says there is a One out there ... why cant there
> be lots of the ones...each fine for the situation and then we move on ... isn't that more
> realistic ... this romantic dream ... it's just like mad ... why do we need this one, this other
> half, I don't need the One to make me whole.'

This clearly represents both a disjuncture with past generations, but also their
generational typical-ness. However, these views were not typical for all the students.
Two groups emerged that did see marriage and parenthood as important and a source
of meaning. One of the groups was the Asian students who all saw marriage (and
arranged marriage at that) as vitally important and that parenthood was not only
inevitable, but desirable. None of them saw this as blind conformity to parental
wishes or family traditions, but rather as an opportunity to 'be different' (Waheeda)
and 'to make their own difference' (Nazia).

> Shalina: I want the kids, the marriage and not just because it is expected of me ... I want
> that opportunity to be like ... responsible, to nurture, to create ... but everyone seems to
> think that's a bad choice ... that somehow I need freedom to be wild, to live, to do what?
> Drink, drugs, have lots of sex ... what used to be seen as growing up is now to be like ... I

dunno ... avoided like the plague, put off for some future point ... like it catches up with you or something.

Creativity, meaning and faith all merged together for Syed in his impending fatherhood.

> Syed: Being a dad matters ... it is the one thing that has real meaning ... it is beautiful ... it is creation and so much more than wanting ... wanting ... wanting ... we've been talking about meaning search but for me raising my son is my meaning ... my goal ... my purpose, everything else is just shit to deal with.

In addition a small number of the non-Asian students, particularly the males, put forth the view that if they did choose parenthood and marriage it would be in order to 'do better than their own parents and to make a difference to their child's lives' (Joe). There was also a sense of meaning search through the raising of children: 'I'll find out who I really am as a man.' (Paul). Again, the risks of marrying in a world where marriage seems doomed to failure, might be worth it for meaning provision and identity formation. Similarly, although the majority of students (and perhaps society in general) sees the raising of children as beset with risks; some might see it as the ultimate risk to be embraced for the benefits of personal growth.

Reverts and Reversals

The six Muslim students were more aware, than their peers, of the limitations and restrictions imposed by family and faith on their lives. They all had more of a sense of responsibilities to others that were not necessarily by choice: unlike their peers the rejection of responsibilities was a greater risk than conformity. All six identified the problems with growing up 'different' in a secular society. All discussed the problems of constantly moving between different cultural milieus. While teenagers all had rebelled against their family, most notably through the rejection of their religion. However, all agreed that while at university all had reversed this position and gone back to faith, some more than others. For Syed impending fatherhood[5] had made him reflect on his values and who he was and he realised that his faith was more permanent and important than the things he had once seen as meaningful. He had risked the condemnation and mockery of his friends to revert back to the values of his childhood:

---

5 It should be noted that Syed's family had rejected him on discovering that his non-Muslim girlfriend was pregnant with his child. The couple are not married. Thus, although fatherhood is an important aspect of being an adult Muslim man, Syed's fatherhood was not welcomed by his parents as it traversed religious and cultural rules.

nobody really gets it…but foundations need to be there and Islam does that for me. The fancy car, the money, the job … it's not going to make us all happy, there's got to be more going on … Islam is that more for me.

Shalina and Nazia went further than Syed by actively embracing a far more tradition Islam than their parents; indeed both had faced parental opposition from adopting the hijab, wearing traditional dress and had become very involved in their local mosques. In becoming 'reverts' they had found both a strong central identity source and ontological security. Both identified contemporary society as devoid of meaning and purpose, as Shalina notes:

It's this race to be … to get … to want more … but why? Why should we all follow this path…it hasn't made me any happier in that deep sense … Islam for me does that … I have direction, I have purpose … no one seems to get it … everyone's like why stand out … is this cos of 9/11 … are you a radical … but you know it's about me, its not political, It's not being showy … its about saying 'I don't have to do things just to be like everyone else.'… there's a bigger picture.

Nazia, echoing Shalina, went on to say:

we talk a lot about risks, real risks, terrorism, unemployment, the hole in the ozone layer…but what of the risk of not living your life in a meaningful way … how empty … how sad … my faith makes me whole … I don't need the other stuff.

The reversion to faith or at least the shift back towards it was a marked characteristic of all six Muslim students. Although this must be contextualised in a post-9/11 world, none of them identified that as the main reason for these reversions. Rather they were about meaning search and making a difference at an existential level. Like their non-religious peers, the risk was in not reversing, but in staying put within a secular, consumerist shaped model of identity. While some of the students saw travel as a voyage of self-discovery, meaning and critique of contemporary society, then the 'reverts' saw going back to faith in much the same way. As Nazia noted:

I'm praying much more now and reading and thinking … sometimes my mind is just buzzing as I see the possibilities and uncover so many new things about myself.

In group discussions the topic of reversion provoked amongst the students strong debates about the need for meaning at a spiritual level; a sense of there needs to be 'something above and beyond us' (Faz). All of them saw the 'sense' behind the reversions, and most of them identified the need for something spiritual in life. This is significant as the majority of the students had self-identified as 'non-religious'. This discourse of 'something more out there' was not associated with any traditional forms of religion, but rather identified the need for a spiritual outlook in the broadest sense. This spiritual outlook identified a number of key aspects to a meaningful life: holistic living, being ethical, making a difference, personal growth and thinking beyond the everyday. In this we can see a strong New Age-infused form of spirituality (Heelas 1996). This is unsurprising as New Age discourses permeate contemporary society and intermingle with 'therapy' culture discourses on growth (Bruce 1995; Heelas 1996). One could be cynical that these existential musings are self-centred, focused as they are on personal growth, but once again they demand a rejection of the everyday and accepted way of being. Consumerism is not deemed satisfying in terms of existential meaning, and therefore spiritual exploration is necessary to offset the risk of meaning crisis.

As Tulloch and Lupton (2003) note the 'voluntary' risk taker seeks out risks for a variety of what might be termed immediate gratifications (for example, excitement), but which are underpinned by the desire for self-actualisation or development. The quest to define an authentic 'adult', more 'real' than the superficial economic model, lies at the heart of the behaviours listed above, such as travelling long-term Additionally, and following Tulloch and Lupton (2003), the pursuit of risks provides a means to act, to have agency and fight passivity. In the face of economic realities that suggest 'full' adulthood is a long way off then travelling, parenting or religion are alternative routes of action and meaning.

All four 'risky' strategies show concern with authenticity, meaning, and identity. They also show the importance of contextualisation in relation to risk. For example, the behaviour of the 'reverts' might initially be seen as decidedly unrisky; strong religious faith has often been associated with security, continuity and conformity. However, the families of the 'reverts' wanted their children to pursue the same career and aspiration-driven patterns as their non-Muslim peers. The key difference is that their parents wanted it framed within traditional (and to some extent religious) patterns of family structure and responsibilities. Therefore to revert to a stronger and more defined faith than their parents and in turn reject parent-defined career plans, was indeed risky and a significant form of resistance.

The four strategies identified in this chapter also highlight a rejection and critique of contemporary, economic models of adult identity and the adoption of alternative routes to being. But none of them are viable long-term alternatives; all the students assume that they will be 'sucked back in' (Matt) to the everyday world of debt, conspicuous consumption and status anxiety. These strategies are 'stalling tactics' that are seen to allow them to construct a sense of self that will be robust enough to deal with re-immersion into late modern consumer society. As Cameron put it:

> You can't keep movin' forever ... you've got to stop, get back into the real world ... but when I do that, I'll be doing that with a better sense of who and what I am, what I want and what I don't want ... I'll settle for less because I know better and don't need all that [consumer] shit to either make me happy or define who I am.

Lost in Transition...

Shifting from childhood into adulthood has always been a difficult transition, with different stages along the way that one must negotiate. With modernity, clearer boundaries were established between different life stages (Aries 1996; Stone 1980; Riley and Waring 1988; Vincent 2003). The onset of late modernity has seen a troubling blurring of such boundaries (Foucault 1984; Giddens 1991; Vincent 2003). This blurring has been caused by structural changes, both economic and social, such as the assertion of the rights of children, greater economic dependency on parents, extension of time at school and the expansion of universities. The decline in traditional, usually, ritualistic life-course markers has exacerbated this situation (Bruce 1995; Bell 1997). With this blurring of boundaries have come risk discourses (Beck 1992), where the risks inherent to each life-stage are amplified and provoke over-protective behaviours by care-givers that can merely exacerbate risk-embracing behaviours for many (for example teenage alcohol misuse). While much attention has been on the impact on childhood; adulthood has also been affected. 'Young adulthood' in particular has emerged as a liminal state, where the individual is betwixt and between adolescence and 'full' or 'mature' adulthood. This stage seems to be elongating throughout the twenties perhaps even into the thirties, driven partly by economic and social realities, but also by individuals' responses to this troubling transition phase.

The middle class students in this study are the product of over-protective parents and were raised in risk-aversive environments whilst also dealing with the fragmentation of family life. All of them felt that they were permanently in a state of transition, but how and when they would get 'there' [to adulthood] was open to question. Media discourses exacerbated their sense that where they were trying to get, was increasingly out of reach. Their response to this was to risk it all, by embracing constant travel, working in 'make a difference' low paid or even unpaid jobs and rejecting the career track, the property ladder, and the 'meaninglessness of consumerism. The failure would be to have remained in that society. For those who did not have the option to travel, religion provided a strong identity source, again with strong anti-consumerist discourses. While meaning quest was a significant part of all their worldviews (hardly surprising given their liminal status), so was a 'real world' critique of contemporary society. This echoes Foucault's (1984) view that in late modernity competing discourses produce new forms of agency and resistance. The fluid nature of contemporary young adulthood created risk-embracing behaviours among the students and in doing so contrastive interpretations of 'being adult' emerged, such as, being ethical, taking responsibility, and being a parent; none of which are necessarily new ways of being an adult but perhaps suggest a reiteration or reclaiming of 'adult' as a meaningful category.

The more we infantilise adults and defer adulthood, the more likely we are to further blur the boundaries between the early stages of the life-course, with consequences for all. Such consequences can already be seen in the debates around childhood. Delaying adulthood brings with it a deferring of responsibility and a sense of not having a 'full' place in society. But if the students do not feel part of society; then what issues does that raise for the long-term health of contemporary society? The risk of staying put and accepting the status quo ('good car, good job, nice things' - Steve) is increasingly a risk too far, but brings with it behaviours that could be risky for the long term success of society. Pursuing self-growth or self-exploration as a central goal in life can negate civil and political participation. The students in this study increasingly find themselves, and their peers, in the holding pattern that is 'deferred adulthood' waiting to 'become', and often becoming lost in this state of transition.

References

Aries, P. (1996), *Centuries of Childhood* (London: Pimlico).

Beck, U. (1992), *Risk Society: Towards a New Modernity* (London: Sage).

Beck, U. (1994), 'The Reinvention of politics: towards a theory of reflexive modernization', in Beck et al. (eds).

Beck, U. et al. (eds) (1994), *Reflexive Modernization: Politics, Traditions and Aesthetics in the Modern Social Order* (Cambridge: Polity Press).

Bell, C. (1997), *Ritual: Perspective on the Practice of Religion* (Oxford: Oxford University Press)

Berger, P. et al. (1974), *The Homeless Mind: Modernization and Consciousness* (Harmondsworth: Penguin)

Bruce, S. (1995), *Religion in Modern Britain* (Oxford: Oxford University Press).

Bryman, A. (2001), *Social Research Methods* (Oxford: Oxford University Press).

Carpenter, L. (2007), 'We've never had it so good' *Guardian Unlimited* [website], (updated 11 March 2007) <http://lifeandhealth.guardian.co,uk/family/story/0,,2028537,00.html>

Connell, R. W. (2002), *Gender* (Cambridge: Polity Press).

Foucault, M. (1984), 'What is Enlightenment' in Rabinow P. (ed.) *The Foucault Reader* (Harmondsworth: Penguin).

Furedi, F. (2004), *Therapy Culture: Cultivating Vulnerability in an Uncertain Age* (London: Routledge).

Giddens, A. (1990), *The Consequences of Modernity* (Cambridge: Polity Press).

—— (1991): *Modernity and Self-identity: Self and Society in the Late Modern Age* (Cambridge: Polity Press).

Goldthrope, J. et al. (1968), *The Affluent Worker: Industrial Attitudes and Behaviour* (London: Cambridge University Press).

Heelas, P. (1996), *The New Age Movement: The Celebration of the Self and the Sacralization of Modernity* (Oxford: Blackwell).

Lupton, D. and Tulloch, J. (2002), 'Risk is Part of Your Life: Risk Epistemologies Among a Group of Australians', *Sociology* 36:2, 317–34.

MacKenzie, J. M. (2005), 'Empires of travel: British guide books and cultural imperialism in the 19th and 20th centuries', in Walton, J. K. (ed.).

McDowell, L. (2006), 'Reconfigurations of Gender and Class Relations: Class Differences, Class Condescension and the Changing Place of Class Relations', *Antipode* 38:4, 825–50.

McRobbie, A. (2004). 'Notes On "What Not To Wear" and Post-Feminist Symbolic Violence', *The Sociological Review* 52:2, 97–109.

Newman, D. and Gauerholz, E. (2002), *Sociology of Families* (London: Sage).

Palmer, S. (2006), *Toxic Childhood* (London: Orion).

Rabinow, P. (ed.). (1984), *The Foucault Reader* (Harmondsworth: Penguin).

Riley, M. W. A. and Waring, J. (1988), 'Sociology of Aging', in Smelser, N. J. (ed.).

Roberts, K. (2001) *Class in Modern Britain* (London: Palgrave).

Office of National Statistics (2007) *Social Trends 37* [website] (updated 27 April 2007) <http://www.statistics.gov.uk/cci/nugget,asp?id=178>

Skeggs, B. (1997), *Formations of Class and Gender: Becoming Respectable* (London: Sage).

Smelser, N. J. (ed.). (1988), *Handbook of Sociology* (Newbury Park, CA: Sage)

Stone, L. (1980), *The Family, Sex and Marriage in England 1500–1800* (New York: Harper and Row).

Urry, J. (2000), *Sociology Beyond Societies: Mobilities For The Twenty First Century* (London: Routledge).

Van Gennep. A. (1977), *The Rites of Passage* (London: Routledge and Kegan Paul).

Vincent, J. (2003), *Old Age* (London: Routledge).

Walton, J. K. (ed.) (2005), *Histories of Tourism: Representation, Identity and Culture* (London: Channel View).

Index